Science, History, and the Shroud of Turin

Robert W. Maher

VANTAGE PRESS
New York / Washington / Atlanta
Los Angeles / Chicago

FIRST EDITION

Published by Vantage Press, Inc.
516 West 34th Street, New York, New York 10001

Manufactured in the United States of America
ISBN: 0-533-06641-7

Library of Congress Catalog Card No.: 85-90133

*Science, History,
and the
Shroud of Turin*

To
Mary Jane Maher
and
Anne Maher Stoddard,
without whose many suggestions and gentle prodding
this book would never have been written

Contents

Preface

Another book on the Shroud of Turin? The number of words already expended on this theme is almost as incredible as the story of the Shroud itself. It would seem that the subject has been exhaustively treated by the many excellent books and articles already in print. The books in existence, however, are in most instances not entirely suitable for the general reader because they are couched in scientific terms, cover only a limited aspect of the Shroud story, are religiously orientated, or are not up to date.

This book attempts to provide the moderately interested individual with a concise, yet complete, scientific and historical view of what has been discovered regarding an ancient burial cloth. The reader is encouraged to make his own decision as to whether the Turin Shroud is the actual burial cloth of Jesus Christ. This book attempts to provide all of the pertinent evidence, some strong and others weak, regarding the authenticity of the cloth that some claim is the same piece of linen purchased by Joseph of Arimathea, circa A.D. 33, for wrapping the crucified Jesus.

Rochester, New York
January 1985

Acknowledgments

The author would like to thank the following for giving permission to reprint materials in this book:

Harper's magazine, for permission to reprint extracts from "Shred of Evidence," by Cullen Murphy. Copyright 1981 by HARPER'S Magazine. All rights reserved. Reprinted from the November 1981 issue by special permission;

Us magazine, for permission to reprint an extract from the January 24, 1977, edition;

Doubleday, for permission to reprint an excerpt and illustration from *The Shroud of Turin,* by Ian Wilson;

The *New York Times,* for permission to reprint "The Shroud of Turin" and a letter to the editor;

National Review, Inc., for permission to reprint a column by William F. Buckley, Jr., and extracts from "The Shroud," by Jerome S. Goldblatt;

Mr. Buckley, for permission to reprint the aforementioned column;

Universal Press Syndicate, for permission to reprint an article by William F. Buckley, Jr.;

Hannibal, for permission to use some of their photographs;

The Rev. Vincent J. Donovan, for permission to reprint a letter of his published in the *New York Times;*

The Holy Shroud Guild, for permission to reproduce many photographs; and Macmillan Publishing Company, for permission to reprint extracts from *Shroud,* by Robert K. Wilcox.

Science, History,
and the
Shroud of Turin

Part 1
Photography

The Shroud of Turin, during its (perhaps) two thousand years of existence, has been considered by many—first by the Eastern Orthodox Christians and later (after A.D. 1204) by Roman Catholics—to be an authentic religious relic. Many devout Christians over the centuries have considered this piece of linen to be the actual burial cloth of Jesus Christ. Others, both Christian, and non-Christian, remain skeptical.

A fortuitous event, the photographing of the Shroud in 1898, transformed this religious relic into an archaeological artifact that if not a forgery, profoundly affects our knowledge of the last days of Jesus on earth. For the past eighty-five years, this ancient strip of linen has probably been studied and tested to a greater degree than any art object or other archaeological artifact on record. Modern research on the Shroud began after an amateur Italian photographer, Secondo Pia, photographed the 14½ × 3½ foot Shroud of Turin for the first time, around the turn of the century. He made the startling discovery that the complete frontal and dorsal image of the nude man on the cloth is actually a negative image with photographic qualities. (See Illustration 1, which shows the face area only.) Since the taking of that first photograph, scientific and historical research have uncovered many facts that support the supposition that the Shroud could be the burial cloth of Jesus Christ. It is the purpose of this book to explore the evidence that has accumulated.

1

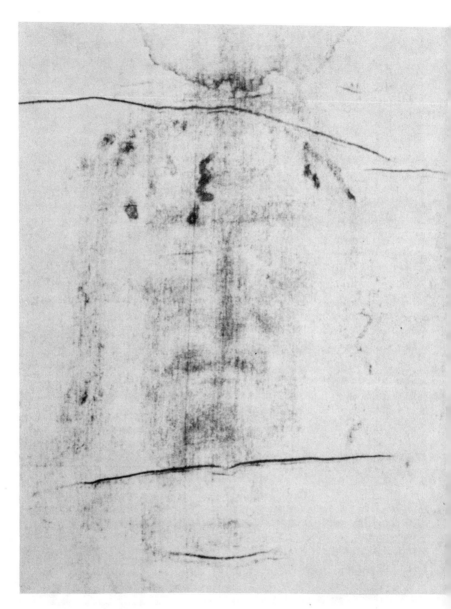

Illustration 1. On the left is the face as it appears on the shroud, and on the right is the face as it appears on a photographic negative.

Holy Shroud Guild

RELIGIOUS RELICS

One of the stumbling blocks for many who become aware of the Shroud has been the fact that it is a religious relic such as some of the other well-known ones: holy nails, wood from the True Cross, the Holy Blood of Bruges, the Index Finger of Saint Thomas the Apostle, and the incredible Holy Foreskin. Roman Catholics, particularly since the Vatican II Council, have tended to downplay the significance of relics. Protestant reaction to religious relics has always been strongly negative. Others (except perhaps some Eastern Orthodox Christians) probably consider most, if not all, religious relics hoaxes. The author does not contemplate the Shroud of Turin as a religious relic, but instead concentrates on the considerable scientific and historical developments regarding the Shroud as an ancient illustration of a significant event. Regardless of religious or nonreligious orientation, the story of the Shroud is a fascinating one, as evidenced by the large number of books, newspaper accounts, and magazine articles written in recent years. The complete story, however, is not an easy one to grasp. This book will attempt to cover various aspects of the Shroud of Turin, one at a time, in order to bring the entire subject into a sharper focus, beginning with photography.

PHOTOGRAPHY DISCOVERED

Historians agree that no one person discovered photography. If any one year can be assigned to the discovery, it probably should be 1839, when in August, Louis Jacques Mande Daguerre, a Frenchman, formally announced his method for producing "daguerreotypes," which consisted of a sheet of copper, plated with silver, exposed in a camera and then processed with mercury fumes. Although this type of photography became very popular and remained so for many years, it was later supplanted by the negative-positive system that we know today. In this latter system, of course, a negative is made on a sensitized film (or paper or glass) in a camera, developed, and subsequently printed on paper in order to produce a positive image, i.e., a print.

William Henry Fox Talbot, an Englishman, learned surreptitiously in January 1839 that Daguerre had succeeded in fixing (making permanent) the image produced by a camera. Talbot, therefore, decided to announce immediately his process for making and "fixing" a negative image from a camera on paper. He, apparently, had not thought of going one step further and transferring his negative image onto another piece of paper and thereby securing a positive print. It remained for Sir John Herschel, another Englishman, to suggest, in March 1839, that the paper negative be waxed (thereby making it transparent) and then put in contact with another piece of sensitized paper to produce a positive image print. Thus within a three-month period, three men working independently announced processes that are now known collectively as photography. None of these men nor anyone else living in 1839 knew that there was in existence a cloth with a negative image "fixed" many centuries before any photographic process had been discovered by man. This cloth, alleged to be the burial shroud of Jesus Christ, lay in a silver box, triple locked within the altar of a chapel, attached to the Cathedral of Saint John the Baptist in Turin, Italy. The cloth is, of course, the Shroud of Turin, so called because it has resided in that city for the past four hundred years, except for a six-year period during World War II when it was hidden in a monastery in Avelino, Italy.

The image on this burial cloth has several unusual characteristics:

1. It has the properties of a photographic negative, which means that light areas are dark and dark areas light and also rights and lefts are interchanged.
2. The image is extremely detailed. The man depicted on the Shroud was apparently severely whipped with an ancient Roman device called a *flagrum*. This whip was tipped with small metal balls that cut into the flesh of the victim. In the wound images from this whip, the microscope reveals scratches from the metal balls.
3. The image has three-dimensional information that makes it

possible to generate, by computer, a 3-D (relief) surface of the body image. This cannot be done with an ordinary photograph or painting without considerable distortion. Three-dimensional reconstructions, however, are possible in stellar and other types of photography where the amount of light received from an object depends upon its distance from the camera.

Because of the above characteristics, it would seem impossible for anyone to have painted the image on the Shroud.

EARLY RESEARCH

Webster's New Collegiate Dictionary defines *photography* as "the art or process of producing images on a sensitized surface (as a film) by the action of radiant energy and esp. light." Those who have tested the Shroud are of the opinion that some energy source produced the image of the body. The Shroud is also stained with blood in all the places that one would expect from the accounts of the Crucifixion. There are the marks of scourging, nailing, and piercing, perhaps by thorns, and a lance wound. These stains, recorded as positive images on the Shroud, of course, become negative images on any photographic negative, such as the one Pia produced in 1898. Pia's approximately 20 × 24 inch negative quickly attracted the interest of scientists, especially medical men. Researchers could now study this early negative and prints from it, which they immediately began to do. The actual Shroud was rarely displayed (three or four times per century), and when it was on view, few persons were able to be near it for any prolonged period of time. The face and body images on the Shroud are not lifelike, but become natural looking only when their light values are reversed, as occurs on a photographic negative. For almost a third of the twentieth century, the rather poor-quality negative made by Pia was the only primary source of information for study of the Shroud by scholars and scientists.

6

In 1931, Giuseppe Enrie, an Italian photographer, was asked to photograph the Shroud without a covering glass, which Pia had to contend with in 1898. Enrie took twelve pictures that are considered to be of superb quality. In addition, Enrie enjoyed the advantages of the considerable technical advances made in photography since 1898, including orthochromatic film, which is sensitive to all colors of visible light except red. He produced strongly detailed black-and-white photographs that are still very valuable for general use and analysis, although inadequate for some of today's more advanced research techniques. More recent photographs using panchromatic film (sensitive to all visible colors of light) produce black-and-white pictures that are better for research purposes, but as a rule do not show as much contrast between the ivory-colored cloth and the brownish image on it and are, therefore, not as pleasing to the eye.

The Pia negative was admittedly of poor quality, and there was the nagging fear that perhaps a hoax was being perpetuated. The far more professionally made photographs produced by Giuseppe Enrie in 1931 are of excellent quality, as evidenced by the fact that they are still being printed today. A commission of expert photographers watched Enrie work and checked every stage of the photographic process. They issued a notarized statement that the pictures were free from any kind of retouching or other special manipulation of the photographic process. Upon publication of the Enrie photographs, all doubt that some sort of photographic fraud was being perpetuated vanished.

The Enrie photographs rekindled interest in the Shroud and made possible more detailed studies of the wounds and the consequent suffering of the man depicted on the Shroud. In 1969, the Shroud was photographed in color for the first time. The results, however, were of poor quality.

THREE-DIMENSION RESEARCH

Although research, both scientific and historical, has been continuous since 1898, it has been particularly prolific since

1974, when two young United States Air Force scientists, Drs. John Jackson and Eric Jumper, began an intensive study of the Enrie photographs. They had observed (as Paul Vignon had done at the turn of the century) that the darkness of the image on the Shroud varied inversely with the distance that part of the body was from the covering cloth. They discovered, through the use of sophisticated space-exploration equipment (the VP-8 Image Analyzer, which is used for planetary and stellar photography), that the Shroud included three-dimensional information. When density scan data from the VP-8 Analyzer is fed into a computer, it is possible to produce a 3-D picture on a CRT (television) screen. This led to some important discoveries about the image. The enthusiasm of Jackson and Jumper in pursuing their three-dimensional research attracted some thirty other American scientists and photographers, who banded together to form STURP (Shroud of Turin Research Project), a group that in 1978 was allowed to test the Shroud itself.

THE MOST RECENT RESEARCH

In October of 1978, some forty U.S. and European scientists went to Turin, Italy, to make some 30,000 photographic exposures and perform other definitive, nondestructive tests on this ancient cloth. They used eight tons of equipment, most of which was borrowed from scientific labs in the U.S. This examination was exhaustive; the scientists worked around the clock for five days.

Many wavelengths of energy were used for illumination, from the very short X-rays to the somewhat longer ultraviolet rays, rays including all parts of the visible light spectrum, and various infrared rays. Some of the scientists looked for fluorescence as an indication of the presence of certain chemicals and metals. Others photographed every square inch of the Shroud in black and white and in color, in accordance with a predetermined grid pattern. Many photomicrographs (pictures through a microscope) were made. Light reflected from various parts of the Shroud was split into its component rays, which were photographed.

Much of the photography was accomplished using Hasselblad cameras with 150mm lenses and utilizing Kodak SO-115 film which can be enlarged up to 100 times. Many 35mm cameras using general-purpose and specialized films were also employed. Some excellent color pictures were taken on thirty sheets of a special Polaroid film, about the size of a chest X ray.

FUTURE RESEARCH

In September 1983, Ian Wilson, a historian and chairman of the British Society for the Turin Shroud, called for more definitive tests of the cloth. He made a number of recommendations:

1. The Shroud should be photographed in its entirety including the back of the cloth and its edges that heretofore had been covered with fabric frames.
2. The front of the cloth should be photographed section by section using a large plate camera. This would presumably provide superior definition of at least some areas.
3. The Shroud should be photographed using tangential light photography. This consists of using lighting parallel to or at a small angle from the surface of the object photographed. This type of photography reveals imperceptible surface flaws and anomalies.
4. The cloth should be rephotographed using X-ray, ultraviolet, and infrared film by qualified art-gallery or museum personnel, i.e., by persons experienced in the testing of art and/or artifacts.
5. Additional photomicrographs should be taken by art-gallery or museum personnel.
6. An expert in the history of ancient and medieval textiles should be included on the testing team.
7. A study should be made of microscopic surface debris other than pollen.

8. Analyses of the body and blood images should be made with a traveling binocular microscope in order to locate truly representative image-bearing areas from which very small samples would be excised for microscopic and chemical study.
9. The cloth should be radiocarbon dated.

These and other recommendations undoubtedly will be considered by a team of scientists, scholars, and photographers that is being assembled. The School of Photography at Rochester Institute of Technology is furnishing a team of three faculty members, headed by Dr. Ronald Francis. A group in New York City expects to raise $5 million for the pursuit of this project.

STURP has also submitted a proposal for eighty-five new tests. They discovered from their 1978 experiments that there is still much that is not known regarding the Shroud.

Anastasio Cardinal Ballestrero, the archbishop of Turin and custodian of the cloth, will have to decide what scientists, if any, will be permitted to engage in further tests. In making his recommendations to the Vatican authorities, he will be assisted by a church-appointed technical review commission. No date has been set for the convening of such a commission as of January 1985.

CONCLUSIONS

It can be concluded that for all practical purposes, the image of the body on the Shroud of Turin is a photographic negative with three-dimensional qualities. Photography has played, and apparently will continue to play, a major role in solving inherent mysteries of this ancient piece of linen.

Part 2
The Scientists and Historians, an Ecumenical Lot

The first scientist to present research findings concerning the Shroud of Turin was Yves Delage, who was well known for his agnosticism and aversion to anything considered supernatural. In 1900, he, with a small group of scientists, led by Paul Vignon, from the Sorbonne in Paris, began a study of the photographic evidence from the Secondo Pia negative. Delage, a professor of comparative anatomy at the Sorbonne, gave a lecture at the Paris Academy of Sciences in 1902 on the image of Christ visible on the Holy Shroud of Turin. Even at this early date (less than four years after the first picture of the Shroud had been taken), Delage concluded that the image had been created by some physiochemical process while Christ lay in the tomb. He maintained that from a medical point of view, the wounds and other data are so anatomically flawless that it seems impossible for them to have been the work of an artist. He went on to say how pointless it would have been for an artist to paint a negative image and, besides, there was no trace of any known pigments on the cloth.

TURN-OF-THE-CENTURY CONTROVERSY

Delage's lecture immediately generated a considerable amount of controversy. At this time, anticlericalism was rampant in

11

France, especially among the liberal intelligentsia and the scientific community. The secretary of the Academy of Scientists refused to publish the full text of Delage's lecture, and many of his colleagues felt that Delage had jeopardized a promising career. In other quarters, however, such as the *London Times, Le Figaro* in Paris, and the *Lancet,* a British medical journal, the lecture was given favorable comment.

Later, Delage wrote to the editor of the *Revue Scientifique:* "I have been faithful to the true spirit of science in treating this question [of the Shroud], intent only on the truth, not concerned in the least whether it would affect the interest of any religious party. . . . I recognize Christ as an [*sic*] historical personage and I see no reason why anyone should be scandalized that there still exist material traces of his earthly life." *

ART-HISTORY RESEARCH

The leader of the Sorbonne group, mentioned previously, Paul Vignon, a Roman Catholic, published, in 1902, the first book based on the Pia negative. Vignon was a biologist and art historian who later became a professor of biology at the Institute Catholique in Paris. Although his vaporgraph theory† on the formation of the image was later found to be untenable, his research into some fifteen markings on the face of the Shroud is still used today. These same markings are also found in many paintings, mosaics, frescos, and icons of Christ, beginning with those produced in the sixth century. This analysis proved eventually to be of inestimable value in tracing the history of the cloth. The Vignon markings will be covered in more detail in a subsequent part of this book.

*Excerpt from *The Shroud of Turin* by Ian Wilson. Copyright 1978 by Ian Wilson. Reprinted by permission of Doubleday & Co., Inc.

†This theory postulates that the myrrh and aloes used in ancient Jewish burial rites might sensitize the burial cloth. Morbid sweat from a tortured body will in time produce ammonia, which could possibly affect a sensitized cloth.

THE IMPORTANCE OF PHOTOGRAPHS FOR RESEARCH ON THE SHROUD

When Vignon, Delage, and their Sorbonne colleagues were conducting their early research into the authenticity of the Shroud, their only reference source was the 1898 Pia negative and prints made from it. The Shroud itself remained locked in its reliquary in Turin, Italy, until 1931.

The Shroud at this point gained some acceptance among medical men. With the publication of the Enrie photographs, taken in 1931, the Shroud found renewed and much wider acceptance within the European medical community.

MEDICAL EVIDENCE

The first and perhaps best known of the medical researchers was Dr. Pierre Barbet, a devoted Catholic, a surgeon at Saint Joseph's Hospital in Paris, and author of the book *A Doctor at Calvary,* which is generally considered the seminal work in regard to the medical evidence from the Shroud. Barbet's book, published in 1950, was the result of fifteen years of labor, including many anatomical experiments on cadavers, archaelogical research into the practice of crucifixion, and scriptural studies of the New Testament and other ancient sources. He verified, from the Enrie photographs, the anatomical accuracy of the image—such as the length of the arms and legs as related to the torso et cetera. He also found that the bloodstains, clots, and flow of blood were what one could expect from the wounds that were inflicted according to the Gospel accounts of the crucifixion.

By the use of cadavers, Barbet discovered that nails driven through the palms of the hands will not support a body hung on a cross. The weight of the body will cause the hands to tear away from the nails. The photographs show that the nails driven into the man shown on the Shroud went through the area where

13

the hand meets the wrist—an area where there is enough bony structure to prevent a tearing away. The New Testament, as commonly interpreted, states that Jesus was nailed through the palms of his hands. However, the Greek word that was used in the original is *cheir,* which can be translated to mean "palm," "wrist," or "forearm." Artists following the New Testament account have traditionally depicted Christ as being affixed to the cross with nails through the palms. The recent evidence, therefore, indicates that the Shroud's image is correct and that much Christian art is not, in this minor respect.

It should be noted that the emperor Constantine abolished crucifixion in the Roman empire in the fourth century A.D. Art scenes depicting Christ nailed to the cross did not appear for hundreds of years, by which time, in all probability, artists were not acquainted with the details of this brutal method of execution.

Barbet also discovered and researched the fact that each hand includes only the fingers, with no thumbs being visible. He found that if a spike is driven between the radius and ulna bones in the wrist, the ulnar nerve will in all probability be damaged. This will cause the thumb to flex into the palm of the hand. From the Shroud image, it appears (on the one wrist that can be seen) that a spike was driven through the wrist in the radius-ulna area.

Barbet noted that there are two blood flows from the wrist wound shown on the Enrie photographs. One flow would have occurred when the man on the Shroud was in a somewhat sagging position and the other when he pushed himself up into a straightened position in order to facilitate breathing. Barbet concluded that the man of the Shroud died from asphyxia when he no longer had the strength to push himself up on the nail through his feet.

ARCHAEOLOGICAL EVIDENCE

In 1968, some 18 years after the publication of *A Doctor at Cavalry,* archaelogists, working in an excavation of an ancient cemetery in Jerusalem, found the skeleton of a crucified man. The man, named Yohanan Ben Hagalgol (taken from an inscription on his ossuary), is believed to have died about A.D. 70. There were nail holes through his wrists. The radial bone at this point was worn smooth, probably by friction as Yohanan pushed himself up in order to breathe and then sank down again because of the pain from the nail through his feet and fatigue of the lower limbs. Yohanan probably died in the same way as the man of the Shroud, because his legs were broken at some point during his crucifixion and he could, of course, no longer push himself up in order to make it possible to exhale. Archaeology has confirmed the record on the Shroud and Barbet's experiments, as described in his book, both in regard to where the arms were nailed and the seesaw motion of a person on a cross trying to breathe. Yohanan's skeleton was the first and only one discovered of a person that had been crucified by the Romans. The Romans ordinarily cast the remains of crucified persons into a lime pit where the corpses would be completely destroyed. (Crucifixion was usually reserved for slaves and the worst types of criminals. Roman citizens were supposedly exempt from this type of execution.)

RECENT MEDICAL RESEARCH

Barbet was followed by many other medical men, such as Professor Hermann Mildder, a radiologist from Cologne, Germany, who experimented on living students suspended by their arms in order to determine the effects of crucifixion; Dr. Giovanni Judica-Cordiglia, professor of forensic medicine at the University of Milan, who studied how image and bloodstains were transferred from the body onto the Shroud; and Dr. David Willis, a general practitioner in England who collated and evaluated all the research available prior to 1974. Dr. Willis was foremost among medical men in refuting the claims of Kurt Berna, a German author who claimed that the Shroud proves Christ did not die on the cross. In the United States, Dr. Anthony Sava of Brooklyn studied the bloodstains, particularly of the wound in the side. Dr. Robert Bucklin, a pathologist and deputy medical examiner of Los Angeles County, has made postmortem examinations of the Shroud photographs. He is convinced that the image is authentic in regard to depicting death by crucifixion. He stated that "the Shroud of Turin Research Project never intended to make a determination of the validity of claims that the Shroud is the burial cloth of Jesus. Such is not within the realm of science, but may be decided by careful historical inquiry. All that was ever proposed to be done by the scientists was the most complete and impartial scientific investigation possible under the circumstances of the study. . . . The interpretation of the findings was intended to be left to each individual who might be concerned with it." *

Not all of the medical researchers agree with Barbet that death was the result of asphyxiation. Bucklin says congestive heart failure was the cause of death. Another medical doctor, Frederick Zugibe, chief medical examiner of Rockland County and an associate professor of pathology at Columbia University, says cardiac and respiratory arrest due to shock were the primary basis for death. All three, however, agree that the man depicted on the Shroud was crucified and that rigor mortis can be detected in the image. In other words, for the layman at least, the doctors are merely quibbling over details in regard to the cause of death.

TESTING BREAKTHROUGH

From the days of Delage until June of 1969, scientists with a serious interest in the Shroud were unable to gain access to it and all studies had to be based on photographs. There had been pressure for many years from the United States Holy Shroud Guild and its spokesmen, Father Otterbein and Father Rinaldi, to allow testing of the actual cloth. The breakthrough came when Michele Cardinal Pellegrino, the archbishop of Turin, appointed the Turin Commission, comprised of eleven people. Although the cardinal could have obtained men and women of the highest

*Stevenson and Habermas, *Verdict on the Shroud*, (Ann Arbor, Mich.: Servant Books, 1981), p. 189.

eminence in their fields, his choices ranged little further than the Italian Piedmont region. The people chosen were selected for their particular academic expertise. The commission was made up of the following:

5 scientists
3 priests
1 art-gallery director
1 museum curator
1 representative of Umberto II, owner of the Shroud

Most of the people selected were Catholic, but there was an agnostic and a Waldensian Protestant. Giovanni Battista Judica-Cordiglia, a son of one of the members of the commission, was chosen to photograph the Shroud in color for the first time.

The commission determined that the Shroud was in an excellent state of preservation, that there were no dyes or pigments in the image areas, and that the image lay on the very topmost fibers of the threads of the cloth. The removal of minimal samples of the cloth for additional testing under the microscope was recommended. This was done in 1973. Two thread samples and two small pieces of cloth were given to Professor Gilbert Raes, a Belgian of the Ghent Institute of Textile Technology. Other thread samples were given to Professor Giogio Frache, director of forensic medicine at the University of Modena. Also given thread samples were Professors Rizzati and Mari of the forensic department at Modena University. None of the thread removals did any apparent damage to the Shroud. Raes's findings indicated that the cloth was woven in the Middle East.

Perhaps the greatest contribution made by the Turin Commission was that it began to interest top-level scientists in studying the Shroud. It also indicated that much serious scientific work needed to be done. It now became apparent that the Shroud is far more complex than had originally been believed.

POLLEN RESEARCH

In 1973, Dr. Max Frei, a Swiss Zwinglain Protestant, a botanist by training and, until his recent retirement, the head of the Zurich Police Scientific Laboratory, was asked, with others, to come to Turin in order to authenticate the photographs of the Shroud taken by Judica-Cordiglia in 1969. Frei, therefore, had an opportunity to view the cloth at close range. He noticed that the surface of the Shroud was covered with minute dust particles. (Frei had an international reputation for analysis of microscopic substances in his police work.) He asked and was granted permission to remove some of these particles for microscopic examination. He took his samples by pressing small pieces of clear adhesive tape on the cloth. Under the microscope, Frei found that this dust, accumulated over the centuries, included mineral particles, fragments from hairs and fibers of plants, spores from bacteria and nonflowering plants, and pollen from flowering plants. Frei found the pollen to be of great interest, because these grains retain their characteristics for thousands of years and each genus of plant has a different pollen appearance. An analysis of the pollen grains, therefore, makes it possible to deduce the geographic regions in which an object has been exposed to the open air. The pollen that is the most useful, of course, is that from plants that have a limited geographical distribution. Frei's findings were that the Shroud had at some time during its existence been in Palestine, Turkey, and Western Europe.

THE 1974 CONFERENCE

Meanwhile, back in the United States in 1968, a youthful physicist and air force captain, Dr. John Jackson, became interested in the Shroud's negative image. What intrigued him was that the image appeared to have been created at a distance, i.e., by some forms of rays from the body rather than by direct contact of the body with the cloth. He noted the finely graded tones of the image and felt that research was needed to determine the distances (between body and cloth) involved in the image formation. In 1974, Dr. Jackson, along with his friend, Dr. Eric Jumper, an aerodynamicist and also a United States Air

18

Force captain, set up a modest research project in the air force weapons laboratory in Albuquerque, New Mexico. By 1976, they had attracted some thirty highly qualified scientists, engineers, and photographers, who formed the previously mentioned STURP. Originally, about half of the project members lived in New Mexico and the largest single bloc worked at the Los Alamos National Laboratory, located some sixty miles from Albuquerque. Most of the other participants worked at some other scientific outpost of the military-industrial complex, such as the Jet Propulsion Laboratory, the Santa Barbara Research Center, or the Lockheed Missiles and Space Center. One wag asked, "What are they trying to do, blow up the Shroud?" Within the group, there were Protestants (64 percent), agnostics (17 percent), Roman Catholics (11 percent), and Jews (8 percent). Many scientists were cynical about the efforts of STURP. Ray Rogers, a chemist and archaeologist, said when he joined the project, "Give me twenty minutes and I'll have this thing shot full of holes." The minutes have lengthened into years. Since 1978, Rogers has been studying, in his spare time, small threads and hundreds of microfibrils that had been removed from the cloth itself. Rogers's attitude is typical of that of STURP members, who are primarily interested in discovering whether the Shroud is "for real." One member said, "It is just a darn fine project."*

According to *Harper's* magazine, "none of them [STURP members] has a professional stake in the investigation. They are simply dogged personalities cursed with a passion akin to dipsomania for puzzles, and unwilling, by and large, to conclude that any problem can stump them for long."

In March of 1977, Jackson and Jumper organized the United States Conference of Research on the Shroud of Turin. The purpose of this conference, held in Albuquerque, New Mexico, was to evaluate the results of the studies made in 1969 and 1973 in Turin, but a considerable number of additional

*Cullen Murphy, "Shreds of Evidence," *Harper's* magazine, November 1981, p. 44. Copyright © 1981 by Harper's Magazine. All rights reserved. Reprinted from the November 1981 issue by special permission.

findings by STURP and by European scholars who attended were also presented. The conference endorsed the proposal that the Shroud be further tested when it was next displayed, which was planned for the late summer and early fall of 1978. This was subsequently done.

Kenneth E. Stevenson, the editor of the proceedings of the Albuquerque conference, wrote in part:

> In fact, just the way in which so many different papers (26 in all) from various authors complement each other is unusual to say the least. Men from several denominations, myriad backgrounds and two different continents have combined their efforts in an attempt to bring the Shroud out of obscurity and into the public eye. Time, money, equipment, and expertise have been volunteered in an unprecendented way. Along the way, people have responded with enthusiasm to the entire project as if it were their own.
>
> In fact, the project has broken down many barriers. Nonbelievers have trod enthusiastically in the footsteps of Delage seeking the truth of the Shroud. Protestants and Catholics have put aside their differences and stood together in awe before this Holy Relic.*

Jackson and Jumper received, from the first, considerable assistance from Father Adam Otterbein and Father Peter Rinaldi, who had been laboring for many years to have the Shroud tested for authenticity. Father Rinaldi was born in Italy and grew up in the Turin area, where he performed the duties of altar boy at the cathedral. It was here in1931 that he first saw the Shroud. Although he became an American priest, with a parish near New York City, he continued his quest to prove the authenticity of what he believes to be the burial cloth of Jesus.

*Proceedings of the 1977 U.S. Conference of Research on the Shroud of Turin, pps. 241-242.

EXHAUSTIVE TESTING

After the Albuquerque conference, Father Rinaldi, Drs. Jackson and Jumper, and a few of their colleagues flew to Turin in order to put forward their proposals for testing the Shroud to the newly appointed archbishop Anastasio Ballestrero. The archbishop agreed that it could be tested in October of the following year (1978), after a six-week public display of the cloth to celebrate its coming to Turin four hundred years ago. After a year and a half of intensive preparation, the Shroud of Turin Research Project team arrived in Turin with their seventy-two crates of analytic tools of modern science, worth about $2.5 million and weighing eight tons. After some difficulties with the Italian customs officials, the crates were finally delivered to the Renaissance palace of the House of Savoy, the deposed royal family of Italy. This palace, now a national museum, is connected by tunnel with the chapel where the Shroud is kept. The testing took place in a magnificient reception room in the palace, on a specially constructed table, specifically designed to hold the Shroud without any damage to it. Most of the scientists, some forty in all, believed at the beginning that the tests would reveal that the Shroud was not authentic. What they did find will be discussed, in more detail, later in this book.

Not only was there much scientific testing of the Shroud during the 1970s, but the results of significant historical research also came to fruition at that time. In May 1977, Ian Wilson, a British historian and one-time agnostic, published his book *The Shroud of Turin*, later made into a movie called *The Silent Witness.* In this volume, the history of the Shroud was traced from New Testament days to the present for the first time. Prior to this book's publication, the known history of the cloth went back only to the 1350s, when it was displayed in a church in Lirey, a small town near Paris. The prior lack of early history of the Shroud led credence to the rumor that the image was some type of medieval forgery. It was only in the twentieth century that both science and history were able to clearly demonstrate that whatever the Shroud is, it is not a medieval painting or forgery.

The study of the Shroud in the past eighty-five years has attracted a large number of people of many disciplines and many faiths. Of these, a goodly proportion set out to prove the Shroud to be some sort of a clever fake or forgery. Others were determined to demonstrate that the Shroud is a photograph of Jesus at the moment of resurrection. Regardless of personal views, however, the driving force of those researching the Shroud has, in the main, been to determine what it is—fake, forgery, or a fifth gospel, supporting and enlarging upon the suffering death and burial of Jesus Christ as recorded in the New Testament.

Part 3
The Turin Shroud
and Other Ancient Grave Cloths

The New Testament tells us that on the day when Christ was crucified: "When it was evening there came a rich man from Arimathea named Joseph who also was a disciple of Jesus. He went to Pilate and asked for the body of Jesus. Then Pilate ordered it to be given to him. And Joseph took the body and wrapped it in a clean linen shroud and laid it in his own new tomb which he had hewn in the rock; and he rolled a great stone to the door of the tomb and departed." * Illustration 2 shows Jesus being wrapped in a shroud. Linen is an extremely durable substance, as can be attested by the fact that burial cloths similar to the Shroud of Turin have been found that date as far back as B.C. 1500. Some of these early cloths, from Egyptian tombs (of Sethos I, Ramses III, and Queen Makeri), are woven in the same three-to-one twill pattern as the Turin Shroud. (See Illustration 3.) This type of weave is accomplished by having the weft (horizontal) thread pass alternately over three and under one of the warp (vertical) threads. This produces diagonal lines, which were woven to reverse direction at regular intervals (every ten or twelve centimeters) in order to produce the herringbone pattern. A cloth of this type is somewhat more costly to manufacture than a simple one-over, one-under style of weave. Ex-

*Matthew 27:57–61.

Jesus Placed in the Shroud

Holy Shroud Guild

Illustration 2 shows an artist's conception of how Jesus' body could have been wrapped in a fourteen-foot shroud.

Turin Shroud Weave

Illustration 3 is an enlarged section of the Turin Shroud that illustrates the herringbone twill weave.

amples of the more complex three-to-one twill in silk have been found in Palmyra, dated A.D. 276 or earlier, and in England circa A.D. 250.

AN EXPENSIVE PIECE OF PRIMITIVE LINEN

Professor Gilbert Raes of the Ghent Institute of Textile Technology, who was given samples of the Turin Shroud, believes that it could have been woven in the first century A.D. in Palestine. This weave, however, was commonly used in many locations and over many centuries; therefore, the weave is not significant in determining the date and place of manufacture. The weave does indicate that the Turin Shroud was an expensive piece of primitive linen cloth. It also is of generous proportions, fourteen feet and three inches long by three feet and seven inches wide.

COTTON IN THE LINEN

Professor Raes also examined samples of the Turin Shroud under the microscope, using polarized light for the best possible contrast. He verified that both the main portion of the Shroud and its side piece are linen. (The side piece, about three inches wide, was sewn to the main piece with linen thread.) He found that in the main piece, there were unmistakable traces of cotton, which he attributed to the shroud's being woven on a loom that had previously been used for weaving a cotton fabric. The cotton fibers found in the Shroud correspond to a species of cotton that is characteristic of the Middle East. Cotton is not grown in Europe, which indicates that the fabric of the Shroud was in all probability manufactured somewhere in the Middle East.

The professor also analyzed the characteristics of the main portion and the side piece. He found that the type of weave used for both was identical, but the diameter of the thread in the side piece is larger and there are no traces of cotton in the side piece.

It should also be mentioned that the side piece is not quite as long as the main section. There is a theory that the side piece was added after the image was formed in order to balance the face on the cloth. Without the side piece, the image is not centrally located on the cloth. The significance of this addition will be covered later in this book.

The cloth bears many signs of having been manufactured in a primitive way. There are imperfections in the pattern and the weave. The thread was made manually on a spindle rather than on a spinning wheel, which was not introduced in the West until the fourteenth century A.D. There are variations in the diameter of the individual handspun threads. The weave is relatively tight, and it is still supple and strong. The cloth shows no signs of mildew, although it was stored in many dark and damp churches and chapels during its existence. This may be attributable to the fact that in ancient times, linen was bleached with soapwort, which made the cloth more pliable and resistant to mildew, mold, and decay. Around A.D. 600, this method of bleaching was discontinued.

DISFIGUREMENTS OF THE CLOTH

There is no doubt that the ivory-colored, almost yellow with age, Shroud of Turin is an ancient piece of linen cloth. Over the centuries, it has been disfigured in several ways, the most prominent being the burn marks from a fire in 1532. (This fire destroyed the Sainte Chapelle of Chambery, France, where the Shroud was maintained.) At the time of the fire, the Shroud was folded and stored in a silver box. The flames melted some of the silver, which dropped onto the cloth and burned holes in a regular pattern as it progressed through the various layers. The damage was mended with patches of a lighter material; however, it was not possible to remove the scorch marks and they are visible around the repaired work. Water, used to extinguish the fire, stained the Shroud with marks resembling rough-cut diamonds. (See Illustration 4.) There are also deep creases in the cloth, attributable to its being folded in different ways over the centuries.

(Positive and Negative Photograph)

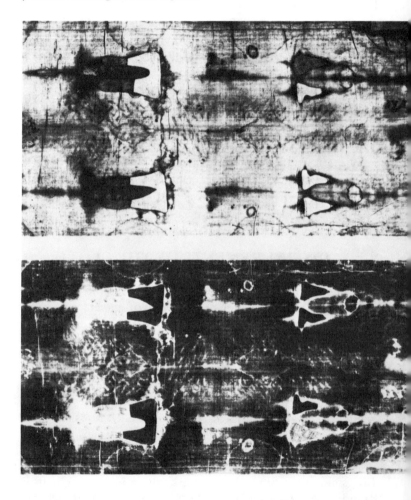

Illustration 4 shows the complete body (top) as it appears on the Shroud and (bottom) as it appears on a photographic negative.

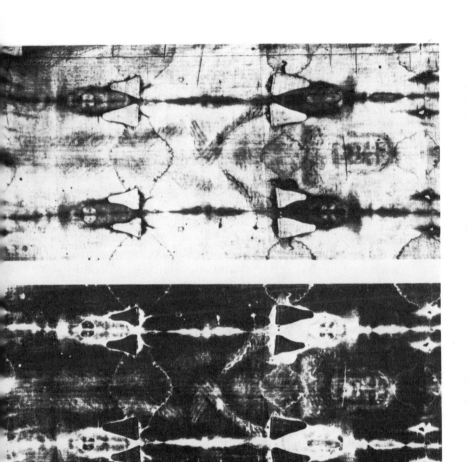

Holy Shroud Guild

Photographed by Vernon Miller ©, Brooks Institute STURP, October 10, 1978, Turin, Italy

IMAGES ON THE CLOTH

Between the two lines of scorch marks and the patches are two images of a body—one frontal and one dorsal—almost joined together at the top of the head. The body images can be described as yellow in color, while bloodstains also present are a dark red. (An excellent color photograph of the Shroud can be found in *National Geographic* June 1980, page 740.)

A JOURNALIST'S FINDINGS

In the early 1970s, Robert Wilcox, the religious editor of the *Miami News,* became interested in the Shroud and wrote a number of articles about it. He was invited to Turin in 1973 to view the Shroud at a time when it was shown on European television. He later spent two years interviewing scientists, historians, and anyone else in Europe and the United States who Wilcox felt knew anything about the Shroud. He was particularly interested in discovering if any other linen burial cloths were imprinted with body images. He sorted through some 200 cloths, dating back to the second century A.D., from the Coptic section of the Louvre Museum in Paris. He found no images, but some decomposition stains. What he also found was a collection of sophisticated weaving patterns that included herringbone, dating back to A.D. 130. Wilcox also contacted several European authorities on burial cloths, and none could tell him of any shrouds with a human image imprinted thereon, except of course for the Shroud of Turin.

Wilcox, who has been described as a former crime reporter and hardened religious skeptic, went on to write a book titled *Shroud.* He was two-thirds through his manuscript before he came to the same conclusion Delage had come to some seventy-five years earlier: "This cloth wrapped the historical person Jesus. I think I proved that." *

*Us magazine, January 24, 1977, p. 29.

DATE OF MANUFACTURE

The most obvious test, which remains to be done on the Shroud, is to date it. This, of course, can be done by the carbon-14 dating process, which requires the destruction of a small sample of material. The amount of material required for the sample has been declining over the years as this process has been increasingly refined. In 1950, some 1,600 square centimeters of material such as linen were needed. By 1974, the area was reduced to twenty-five square centimeters or about ten square inches. In 1977, a revolutionary method of carbon dating was developed at the University of Rochester. Professor Harry Gove, director of the university's Nuclear Structure Research Laboratory, offered to do this dating with a thread from the Shroud, eight inches or one to two centimeters long. This quantity of material, when burned, would provide enough carbon for several tests. This new technique used the university's tandem Van de Graaff accelerator, which would measure the amount of carbon-14 directly. Gove estimates that they could establish the age of the Shroud within about 100 years or better. He went to Turin during the 1978 exposition to press his case, but was unable to obtain permission from the archbishop to perform the test.

POLITICS ENTERS THE PICTURE

It should be kept in mind that the Shroud has been owned for centuries by the House of Savoy, the family that produced the kings of modern Italy. In 1946, the Italians held a plebiscite that determined that Italy should become a republic instead of a monarchy. The last king, Umberto II, now deceased, went into exile in Portugal. Before he left his ancestral home in Turin, he provided that the archbishop of Turin was to be in charge of the Shroud and make all the final decisions in its regard. The king, in recent years, approved scientific tests on the Shroud but left the initiative for such tests to the church authorities in Turin. This arrangement apparently was not understood by Dr. Walter

McCrone, a Chicago microanalyst, who accompanied Jackson, Jumper, and Rinaldi to Turin in 1977 to arrange for the 1978 testing of the cloth. McCrone brought information to Turin on the latest carbon-14 methods of testing, which the Italians received with considerable interest.

During his visit, McCrone was approached by a Monsignor Ricci and his assistant, Mary Patrizzi, friends of the former king, Umberto, who at that time was in nearby Geneva, Switzerland. Ricci and Patrizzi told McCrone that they could arrange a meeting with the king, who might very well authorize a carbon-14 test. McCrone, therefore, visited the king. However, he did not inform Father Rinaldi, who was conducting delicate negotiations on the American's behalf in regard as to how the Shroud would be tested. Thus McCrone went over the head of the archbishop. To compound the error, he did not know that Ricci and Patrizzi were prominent royalists, while the newly appointed archbishop was a "man of the people," somewhat in the mold of Pope John XXIII. The new archbishop was then working closely with the communist mayor of Turin in regards to sprucing up the city and making arrangements for the large influx of visitors expected the following year during the exposition of the Shroud. The archbishop certainly did not want to give the impression that he had any royalist leanings, which would have been anathema to the communists. Although Dr. McCrone had a good idea, i.e., the dating of the Shroud, he only succeeded in alienating the people who could have helped him by injecting a political complication into a matter that should have been decided on scientific and religious grounds.

BROOKHAVEN LABORATORY AND THE UNIVERSITY OF ROCHESTER

At the end of 1978, the Brookhaven Laboratory announced that it could also carbon date, using very small samples. It is hoped that both Brookhaven and the University of Rochester laboratories will be given the opportunity to make these tests independently of each other in order to double-check on the veracity of the results. It is understood that neither the king nor the archbishop was opposed to the use of carbon dating by the new method, but permission has not yet been forthcoming.

THE CLOTH AND THE GOSPEL OF JOHN

On Sunday morning, some thirty-six hours after Jesus was placed in a shroud by Joseph of Arimathea and Nicodemus, Peter entered the tomb: "Then Simon Peter came, following him, and went into the tomb; he saw the linen cloths lying, and the napkin, which has been on His head, not lying with the linen cloths but rolled up in a place by itself." *

The use of the plural *cloths* has caused much controversy among New Testament scholars over many years. Some scholars today believe that the "napkin" referred to by John was not placed on Jesus' face, but was instead rolled up and placed under his chin, and over the top of his head, where it was tied. This would be in accordance with the Jewish burial custom practiced in order to keep the mouth closed before rigor mortis sets in. In like manner, the arms and feet should be bound together according to ancient burial custom.

It is obvious that a "napkin" did not cover the face of the man depicted on the Shroud, because otherwise there would be no facial image on the Shroud. It could, however, have been used as a chin band. There is also indication, on the Shroud image, that there were bindings around the wrists and ankles. It appears, therefore, that the image on the Shroud supports or at least does not contradict John's account of what was found in the tomb on that first Easter morning.

CONCLUSIONS

It can be concluded that it is not unusual for linen to survive for 2,000 years or more. The Shroud of Turin apparently was

*John 20:6–7.

an expensive piece of cloth, of a type that the wealthy Joseph of Arimathea might very well have provided for wrapping Jesus before placing him in the newly hewn tomb. The Shroud probably was woven in the Near East centuries ago, but just how many centuries has not yet been determined. No other shrouds with body images have been found, although many ancient burial cloths from Egypt are in existence. The Shroud of Turin, as a hand-spun, hand-woven, undyed piece of linen, is in close conformity with the New Testament accounts of the burial of Jesus.

Part 4
Blood on the Shroud

There are two types of images on the Shroud. When one is viewing the cloth, the "blood" areas look darker and stand out more sharply than the "body" images, which are mistlike, straw-yellow impressions. Secondo Pia, the first person to photograph the Shroud, noted that the "blood" stains and the image of the man are different. The "blood" stains showed white on his negative, which indicated that they, being dark stains in real life, are a positive image on the Shroud, while the body is a negative image on the cloth. Another difference was noted by STURP, which took part in the testing in 1978. When the backing cloth was loosened, the scientists could see that the "blood" had penetrated the Shroud, while the "body" images were not visible on the back of the cloth. It is obvious that "blood" stains and the "body" images were formed in different ways.

BLOODSTAINS MAGNIFIED

One of the primary objectives of the STURP team was to discover if the "blood" stains are truly blood. By the use of a photomicroscope at thirty-two–times magnification, it was discovered that the blood (or some other substance) spread through the threads of the cloth and was trapped in some places, while in the image areas, only the top fibrils of the threads were affected, like a scorch. In other words, something was added to the Shroud in the "blood" areas, and this something soaked through the cloth at least in some places. It only remained to be determined what the added substance was. The added material has been described as varying between red and reddish-brown, a color that one might expect from old bloodstains when there has been some decomposition.

TESTING THE STAINS

One of the major projects was to determine the composition of the apparent bloodstains by a series of tests, using chemistry and various energy sources for illumination throughout the electromagnetic spectrum, i.e., from X-rays, ultraviolet light, and visible light to infrared light (.16 to 15,000 nanometers of wavelength).

1. Microspectrophotometric Scans of Fibrils

Two of the STURP members, John Heller and Alan Adler of the New England Institute, tested actual Shroud fibrils. These were taken from the surface of the cloth by means of sticky tape. Using fibrils from "blood" areas of the Shroud, they examined, through a microscope, the spectrum of the visual light transmitted from them. They reported in the 1980 *Applied Optics Journal* that hemoglobin was indicated from the colored light transmitted.

2. Ultraviolet Fluorescence

Heller and Adler also removed iron from the fibril samples and attempted to isolate prophyrin, which is the iron component of hemoglobin. They found that iron from the sample fluoresced red under ultraviolet light, which indicated that prophyrin was present. Two other members of the team, Vernon Miller and Samuel Pellicore, studied ultraviolet fluorescent photographs of the "blood" areas. Whole blood does not fluoresce under ultraviolet light. Miller and Pellicori found only a light fluorescence margin around the edges of several of the bloodstained areas. They attributed this to blood serum, a colorless part of blood that probably separated from the whole blood, either before or after the man's death.

3. Chemical Analysis

Fibrils from the white fluorescent areas were mixed with Bromcreosol Green, which gave a positive test for albumin, the principal protein component of blood.

Some of the hardened blood from fibrils was tested using potassium cyanide in ammonium hydroxide. This test also indicated that hemoglobin was present.

A few blood particles had a greenish-brown color. These were tested and indicated bile, which is a decay product of hemoglobin.

4. X-ray Fluorescence

X-ray fluorescence indicated heavy concentrations of iron only in "blood" areas. Iron is an important constituent of the hemoglobin in blood. The X-ray fluorescence also showed that calcium, strontium, and iron were evenly distributed all over the cloth. In the manufacture of linen, it is necessary to soak the flax in water, which loosens the fiber from the woody tissue. This process, known as retting, and in ancient times was done in a pond or lake. During this retting process, the linen fibers act as an ion exchange. It is assumed that the water used to ret the Shroud material contained the calcium, strontium, and iron that had been soaked up by the linen fibers. X-ray fluorescence indicated much more iron in the "blood" area than in the non-"blood" areas.

In STURP's summary of its findings, it was stated that the substance in the bloodstained areas was composed of hemoglobin and tested positive for serum albumin. The scientific tests have determined with virtual certainty that there is blood on the Shroud.

Dr. Walter McCrone, a distinguished Chicago microscopist who demonstrated that Yale's Vinland map is a forgery, disagreed that there is blood on the Shroud. When he looked through his microscope at particles removed from the cloth, he saw evidence of two pigments used in medieval paintings. He made no chemical analysis. When he first announced to the press the results of his findings, he stated, "I am sure the Shroud is a forgery, but I cannot prove it." Later in his own scientific journal, *The Microscope,* he wrote that at the very least, a medieval artist "touched up a pre-existing authentic image on the Shroud." Later he backtracked further in a letter to Ian Wilson, dated May 12, 1981, in which he said: "I don't think any one of us would doubt authenticity if the date of the carbon-14 test came out to be first century." Although Dr. McCrone merely confused the issue, he did incite the STURP scientists to make additional blood tests.

BLOOD AND THE NEW TESTAMENT

Another important question is whether the bloodstains are in conformity with the accounts of Jesus' crucifixion and the events leading up to it as recorded in the New Testament.

We shall begin with the scourging.

> Then Pilate took Jesus and scourged him.
>
> —John 19:1

From the large number of dumbbell-shaped marks on the Shroud, it has been found that the man may have been hit some 120 times with a Roman whip called a *flagrum.* Jewish law limited beatings to forty strokes, but it was the Romans who scourged Jesus. (A *flagrum* was discovered in the ruins of Herculaneum, caused by the eruption of Mount Vesuvius in A.D. 79. These whips consist of a short handle with two or three long leather thongs that have two lead balls (shaped like dumbbells) attached to the end of each thong. The balls are sharp and bite deeply into the flesh of the victim, causing bleeding in many instances from dumbbell-shaped wounds. It was found that the lead balls on an existing *flagrum* fit precisely into the wound marks on the Shroud. (See Illustration 5.) The man of the Shroud was apparently whipped on the back (see Illustration 6), but the thongs would sometimes wrap around the front of his body. The legs and arms also bear wound marks from the whipping, which must have been severe. The man was whipped from both sides by two men, one of whom was shorter than the other, as can be determined by the angle of the wounds. Some pathologists believe that the scourging was the primary cause of death or, at least, hastened it.

> And the soldiers plaited a crown of thorns and put it upon His head and arrayed Him in a purple robe.
>
> —John 19:2

The Shroud shows trickles of blood on the back of the head (see Illustration 7), on the forehead, and in the hair (front view). This would indicate that the crown of thorns was in the form of a cap, such as is customary for crowns in the East. It was not a circlet around the head, as is customarily shown in paintings and statues of Jesus wearing a crown of thorns. Once again, it appears that many works of art may be incorrect in this minor detail, if the man of the Shroud is Jesus. This also indicates that the crown of thorns probably was more painful than artists would lead us to believe by depicting a circlet rather than a cap of thorns. The blood flow on the forehead, in the shape of a reverse 3, indicates that the forehead was lined and contracted, probably by intense pain.

> They came up to Him, saying "Hail King of the Jews": and struck Him with their hands.
>
> —John 19:3

When viewing the Shroud, there appears to be a severe swelling below the right eye, and the cartilage of the nose is

Scourge Marks and Whips

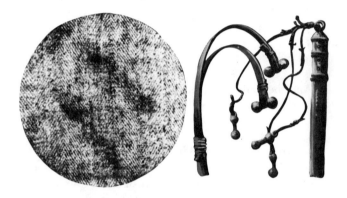

Illustration 5 shows two *flagrums* on the right and an enlarged section of the Shroud with wound marks from a scourging with this type of whip.

Scourge Marks on Back

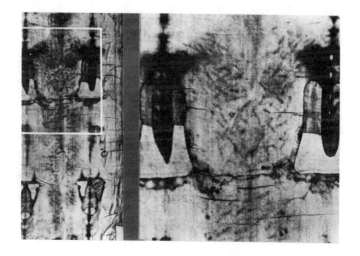

Illustration 6 shows the victim's back covered with wounds from a *flagrum*. The illustration on the right is an enlarged section of the back. On the left is shown the area from the back image that was enlarged. Note that the wound marks on the upper part of the back are blurred, perhaps from carrying a heavy object on the shoulders after the whipping.

Blood on Back of Head

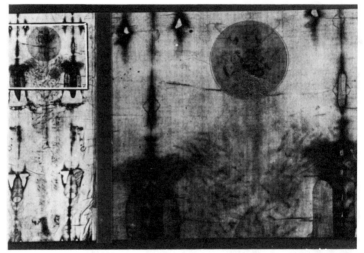

Illustration 7 depicts flows of blood on the back of the head, perhaps from a cap made of thorns.

fractured. There also appear to be other superficial wounds and bruises on the face.

> Then he handed Him over to them to be crucified. So they took Jesus and He went out, bearing His own cross, to the place of the skull which is called in Hebrew "Golgotha."
>
> —John 19:16–17

Modern research into the practice of crucifixion indicates that the victim carries only the crossbeam on his shoulders, tied to his arms with ropes, while the upright beam is already set up at the place of execution. Crossbeams probably weighed in the neighborhood of 100 pounds. The Shroud indicates a mass of tiny lacerations on the shoulders, as though the man had carried a rough, heavy object after the scourging, because the wounds from the whipping are blurred in that area.

> And as they led Him away, they seized one Simon of Cyrene who was coming in from the country and laid on him the cross, to carry it behind Jesus.
>
> —Luke 23:26

Perhaps because of his severe beating, Jesus was unable to carry the crossbeam and, therefore, Simon was pressed into performing this service. The image on the Shroud indicates bruises, swelling, and some dirt in the left knee area, which may have been caused by a fall or falls. The probability that the arms were tied to the crossbeam indicates it would not be possible for the man of the Shroud to use his arms to break a fall. Some of the facial wounds, such as a ruptured nose bridge, swellings on the forehead, cuts over the eyebrow, and minute cuts with blood and dirt on the tip of the nose, may have been caused by falls on the way to the crucifixion site.

> So the other disciples told him "We have seen the Lord," but he [Thomas] said to them "Unless I see in His hand the print of the nails, and place my finger in the mark of the nails, and place my hand in His side, I will not believe."
>
> —John 20:25

The above passage implies that Jesus was nailed to a cross. The image on the Shroud likewise shows that the man depicted there had wounds through his wrists and feet that bled profusely. The wound on the left wrist clearly shows two streams of blood, which were probably caused by changes in position on the cross:—one stream denoting an upright position and the other a slumping position. (See Illustration 8.) When the body was sagging on the cross, it would become difficult for the person to breathe because of the position of the arms. In order to relieve the pressure on the chest, the victim would push himself up on the nail holding his feet. (See Illustration 9.) This change in position accounts for the two streams of blood as recorded on the Shroud. Eventually the victim becomes exhausted, can no longer push himself up, and dies of asphyxiation or cardiopulmonary failure.

> And Jesus uttered a loud cry and breathed his last.
> —Mark 15:37

The swollen abdomen, as shown in the three-dimensional pictures of the Shroud, indicates that asphyxiation was probably the primary cause of death.

> Since it was the day of Preparation, in order to prevent the bodies from remaining on the cross on the sabbath (for that sabbath was a high day), the Jews asked Pilate that their legs might be broken, and that they might be taken away. So the soldiers came and broke the legs of the first, and of the other who had been crucified with Him; but when they came to Jesus and saw that he was already dead, they did not break his legs.
> —John 19:31–33

The legs were broken in order to hasten death, as the victim could no longer push himself up to breathe. The legs of the man shown on the Shroud were not broken.

> But one of the soldiers pierced His side with a spear and at once there came out blood and water.
> —John 19:34

44

Wrist Wound

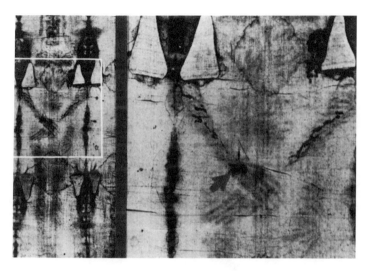

Illustration 8 shows the left wrist wound and the streams of blood down the arm.

Bloody Footprint

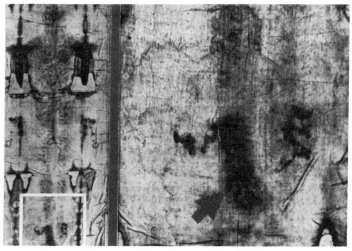

Illustration 9 indicates the footprint in blood from a foot wound.

On the right side of the frontal Shroud image, there is a wound between the fifth and sixth ribs. This wound resembles an elongated oval, about 1 ¾ × ⁷⁄₁₆ inches. The wound, judging from its size and shape, could have been made by a *lancea,* which was a spear that was commonly used by Roman soldiers. There is a massive flow of blood from this wound, seen as a large, dark stain, intermingled with smaller clear stains that might be the "water" referred to by John in the above passage. (See Illustration 10.) Dr. Barbet, the French surgeon, performed experiments on cadavers and found that when he inserted a knife into the heart of a recently deceased person, pericardial fluid (serum) and then blood would issue from the wound. (The pericardium is a conical sac that encloses the heart.) Medical men tell us that because of the many torments that Jesus was subjected to on the first Good Friday, it could be expected that there would be a large quantity of serum accumulated in his pericardium. Dr. Barbet also states that in a recently deceased corpse, there is usually a large quantity of liquid blood in the right auricle of the heart. It was probably pericardial serum (which is nearly colorless) that John reported as "water" issuing from the wound.

On the Shroud, there is a large bloodstain below the oval wound in the side, and some of the blood apparently ran around to the small of the back after the body was placed on the cloth in a horizontal position. At the edges of the bloodstains are places that appear to be stained by serum. There areas fluoresce moderately, while the "blood" areas do not. It is likely that the fluorescent margins are of pericardial serum, which remained separated from the whole blood on the Shroud.

. . . . Nor did His flesh see corruption.

—Acts 2:31

There are no signs of decomposition of the body on the Shroud of Turin.

A number of medical men, over the years, have noted that the reddish-brown stains appear to be anatomically correct, i.e., what one would expect from wounds caused by being stabbed in the side and nailed through the wrists and feet. STURP also

Wound in the Side

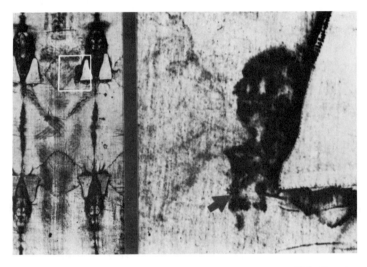

Illustration 10 shows a wound in the side that stained the Shroud with a large quantity of blood and smaller, clear stains which are thought to be pericardial serum. The actual wound cannot be seen in this photograph because it is covered with blood. It can, however, be viewed by the use of certain image enhancement techniques.

noted that the edges of the blood clots are precisely defined, which made them wonder how the body could have been removed from the Shroud without smearing and breaking down the edges of the clotted blood.

CONCLUSIONS

It can be concluded that what appears to be blood clots and stains on the Shroud were caused by blood and were not some pigment or other material added to the cloth. The comparison of the information from the Shroud with the New Testament indicates substantial agreement. In no way can it be demonstrated, from the tests made to date, that the Shroud information is in conflict in any way with the New Testament accounts of the crucifixion and burial of Jesus. On the other hand, the testing does not prove conclusively that the man of the Shroud is Jesus. Carbon-14 dating tests could further establish the authenticity of the Shroud or prove it to be a fraud.

Part 5
The Image on the Shroud

The complete front and rear images of a five foot, ten inch, bearded, unclothed man on this ancient linen cloth are the most enigmatic aspect of the Turin Shroud. The front and rear images appear head to head, as though the body was lying on its back at one end of the Shroud. Then the cloth was drawn over the face and the front part of the body. The hands are crossed over the pelvis.

Professor Carlton S. Coon, the ethnology curator at the University of Pennsylvania, wrote to Robert K. Wilcox: "Here are the pictures [of the Shroud] that you asked me to return. Whoever the individual represented may have been, he is of the physical type found in modern times among Sephardic Jews and noble Arabs. The soft parts of the nose have shrunken a bit, which is simply a sign of death. I have seen the same thing in the mummies of Egyptian Pharaohs."*

The bloodstains, as covered in part 4 of this book, are straightforward in that the scientists were able to identify them as from actual blood that oozed or became smeared on the cloth in places where one would expect to find them after reading the nineteenth chapter of John's Gospel. The body images, however, are mistlike, straw-yellow impressions that seem to fade into the cloth as one approaches it more closely. For the best view of the

*Robert K. Wilcox, *Shroud*, copyright © 1977, by Macmillian Publishing Company, p. 136. Used by permission.

images, one should be fifteen to twenty feet away, in order to allow the eyes to better resolve the detail. This phenomenon, lateral neural inhibition, is well known to painters.

CHARACTERISTICS OF THE IMAGE

As mentioned in part 1, the image has the properties of a photographic negative, which means that light areas are dark and dark areas are light and rights and lefts are interchanged as compared with the real world. The reversal of light tones, of course, causes difficulties when viewing the image on the cloth. When, however, the tones are reversed by photography, it becomes much easier to comprehend the Shroud's image. In addition, it should be recalled that the image, in spite of its mistlike qualities, is extremely detailed—similar to a sharp photograph. It also has three-dimensional qualities that are not apparent to the naked eye but can be brought out by the use of sophisticated imaging equipment. All of the above characteristics were known by the STURP scientists before they went to Turin in 1978 to test the Shroud.

THE SHROUD IN THREE DIMENSIONS

Before describing the tests made in Turin, the three-dimensional aspects of the Shroud image should be considered in some detail. As mentioned before, Drs. Jackson and Jumper conducted the initial three-dimensional research beginning in the early 1970s. Jackson had noted, as had Paul Vignon at the turn of the century, that the darkness of the image seems to vary with the probable distance between the cloth and the body as it lay in the tomb. For instance, the forehead and tip of the nose (which probably touched the cloth) are dark on the Shroud, while the eye sockets and the neck are very light or not recorded to a discernible extent. The hue of each fibril in the image areas is the same as all the other yellowed fibrils. It is the number of yellowed fibrils in a given area that determines the lightness or darkness of the image.

Jackson and Jumper wanted to determine whether there is a definite mathematical relationship between the degree of darkness (opacity) of the different parts of the Shroud image and the distances between the cloth and the body at the instant the image was formed. Their experiment consisted of:

1. placing a man of about the same size as the Shroud man image on a cloth photographic copy of the Shroud;
2. draping a sheet over the reclining figure and recording the distance between the sheet and the man at various points;
3. measuring with a microdensitometer the opacity of the corresponding points (the two above) on a Shroud photograph (negative image);
4. correlating the data from 2 and 3 above, which in graph form appears to correlate very well, i.e., as the distance between body and cloth increases the darkness on the cloth decreases;
5. fitting a curve to the data, which yields the following equation:
$$0 = 9 + 46\, e^{-1.03d}$$
   where 0 = relative opacity
   d = body to cloth distance in centimeters
   e = 2.71828

   (When body-to-cloth distance was greater than four centimeters—about one and one-quarter inches—there is no image discernible on the Shroud.)

The formula above with an Interpretation System VP-8 Analyzer and slides of the Shroud, generated three-dimensional (relief) representation of both the front and back body images.

The VP-8 Analyzer was developed by NASA for producing space photographs from light signals transmitted to earth by space probes. The analyzer incorporates a computer that is programmed to interpret light areas as nearby and dark areas as farther away. It displays the results as a picture on a television screen. It is only when actual nearness (or remoteness) is manifest by more (or less) light that the analyzer can produce an accurate three-dimensional picture. This method of generating a three-dimensional image cannot be accomplished using an ordinary photograph or painting without causing such a large amount of distortion in the resulting image that most viewers would consider it unacceptable.

THE SIGNIFICANCE OF
THREE-DIMENSIONAL RESEARCH

Initially the three-dimensional experiment may not seem to be of much importance, but actually there are some important conclusions to be drawn from it:

1. Authenticity—It would seem to be an impossibility for any artist to have painted the Shroud image as a negative with three-dimensional qualities, based on the distances between various points on the body and the cloth. The three-dimensional qualities support the theory that the image was not manmade, i.e., it occurred by means of a natural (or some may say supernatural) process.
2. Beating and Cause of Death—The large amount of swelling on the right cheek and the extension of the chest and abdomen are apparent in the relief image. This lends credence to the belief that the man was beaten about the face and probably died of asphyxiation on the cross.
3. Leaning Forward—A slight leaning forward and bent knees can be detected in the relief image. It is believed that a body suspended by the arms on a cross would assume a forward lean at the time of death and that the knees would be bent if the body was in a slumped position. These conditions might very well reappear when rigor mortis sets in, because the body tends to assume the same position that it had at the time of death.
4. Coins over the Eyes—It was found that there were button-like objects over the eyelids of the man on the Shroud. It is believed that these are coins. This identification agrees with first-century Jewish burial customs whereby pottery frag-

ments or coins were sometimes placed over the eyes. Coins over the eyes, however, are not limited to the first century A.D. nor to the Jewish culture.

When the right-eye image is magnified, some researchers report seeing the Greek letters "YCAI" and an astrologer's staff. The arrangement of these symbols is such that the "button" on the eyelid appears to be a *lepton*, a ⅝-inch bronze coin minted in Palestine during the period A.D. 26–36, under the administration of Pontius Pilate. The letters on the small coin are about ⅟₃₂ of an inch high. Coins of this mintage are available and were compared with the Shroud image. If this analysis is correct, it would indicate that the image on the cloth was produced at about the time of Jesus' crucifixion, circa A.D. 33. The coin symbols, however, are so small that the weave of the cloth tends to get in the way when an attempt is made to interpret them. Some, therefore, are skeptical as to whether the researchers actually saw what they thought they saw.

5. Cloth Flat over the Body—The Shroud must have lain relatively flat (not tucked in at the sides) over the body when the image was formed; otherwise, there would be considerable distortion in the frontal image. (It should be pointed out, however, that there is some distortion, such as of the fingers of the right hand, which appear to be excessively long.) If the man depicted on the Shroud is Jesus, spices may have been packed along the sides of the body, which could have kept the cloth fairly horizontal over the reclining figure. A large quantity of spices were available and were used, as recorded in John's Gospel: "Nicodemus also, who had first come to Him by night, came bringing a mixture of myrrh and aloes about a hundred pounds' weight. They took the body of Jesus and bound it in linen cloth with the spices as is the burial custom of the Jews."*

All of the image points recorded on the Shroud must have been transmitted in straight lines from the corresponding points

*John 19:39–40.

on the body. The beams also must have been approximately perpendicular (i.e., at right angles) to the cloth. Radiation from an energy source, such as a light bulb, ordinarily spreads in all directions. It is only a laser that radiates beams that are unidirectional and parallel. Under different circumstances, the VP-8 Analyzer would not have been able to produce an undistorted three-dimensional image. In addition, beams from the side of the body, such as the ears, are not recorded on the cloth.

TESTING IN TURIN

When the scientists went to Turin in 1978 to test the Shroud, they had two primary objectives in regard to the image:

1. What is its composition?
2. What process caused its formation?

They, of course, were aware of the three-dimensional research—in particular, the mathematical relationship mentioned above. They also were aware of the hypothesis that the image was caused by a scorch, because in color photographs, the image appears to be the same color as the scorch marks from the fire in A.D. 1532.

UNDER THE MICROSCOPE

When the Shroud is studied under the microscope, at forty times magnification, the individual threads look like stones in a wall and the individual fibrils that make up the threads can be seen. A single thread contains about 200 fibrils. In the image areas, only the topmost two or three fibrils have a yellowish color as compared with the white of the unaffected areas of the cloth. The yellowish color remains the same (has the same color saturation) regardless of the lightness or darkness of the image as viewed with the naked eye. Where the image is dark, such as at the tip of the nose or the middle of the forehead, more fibrils have turned yellow than in areas where the image is light. In other words, the fibrils on the tip of the nose are not a darker yellow than those on the lighter parts of the image; there are just more fibrils that have become yellow. In addition, under high magnification it is apparent that no foreign material plays any part in the makeup of the image, which consists entirely of discolored (yellowish) fibrils.

REFLECTED LIGHT

The linen of the Shroud is cellulose, made from the cell walls of flax plants. It is well known that cellulose turns yellow in the first stages of burning (oxidation). This is observable on old ironing-board covers and also observable on the Shroud around the patches covering the holes caused by the fire of 1532. The scientists found, from reflectance tests using ultraviolet and visible light, that the image and the fire scorches reflect light in a similar way. When plotted on a graph, it appears that the two curves of light reflectance (fire scorch and image) agree within the margins of experimental error. Both curves peak in the ultraviolet region and then gradually decline in the visible light spectrum as wavelength increases (i.e., progresses through the colors from violet to red). The curves, however, are not identical but this may have been caused by the Shroud's being enclosed in a silver box during the fire in 1532, which limited the amount of oxygen available during the scorching and burning of the fabric. It was also found that both the image and the scorch from the fire reduced at a similar rate the overall fluorescence of the cloth.

The scientists noted that neither the heat from the fire nor the water thrown on the cloth to extinguish the blaze had any effect on the image. This is what can be expected from a scorch, but would not be true of pigments, inks, dyes, and other substances that might be used in a painting.

It was also found that the light reflected from the heel was different from the light reflected from the rest of the image.

Low-powered magnification indicated that embedded in the fibers was some dirt—not enough to be seen by the naked eye. Anyone being crucified would, in all probability, not be wearing shoes or sandals. The dirt is perhaps from the area around the foot of the cross. It is doubtful that a forger would add dirt to the heel of his *objet d'art,* particularly when it couldn't be seen.

CHEMICAL TESTING

As mentioned before, the STURP scientists examined thirty-two "sticky tape" samples from the surface of the Shroud during the 1978 tests. These tapes picked up minute particles of metal, synthetic fibers, and linen fibrils. Chemists John Heller and Alan Adler, both of the New England Institute, analyzed some of the yellowed linen fibrils from the image areas. They performed five tests for protein, but found none. Other tests for inorganic compounds found some iron and calcium, but not enough to account for the yellowing of the fibrils. They were also unsuccessful in extracting the yellow color with acids, bases, or organic solvents. It was not possible to bleach the color with strong oxidants. The results of the tests were negative in that they could not find any residual foreign substances that could have formed the image. There also was no evidence of capillary action, like that of a blotter soaking up ink.

Because there was no evidence of capillary action or diffusion of the image, it must be concluded that it was not caused by a liquid or a gas. The intensity of both the front and rear images appears to be the same, although the body appears to have been lying on its back. If the image was the result of body chemicals, the back image would be darker than the front image—or so it would seem.

In a positive sense, the scientists concluded that the fibrils in the image areas were dehydrated (oxidized), while those in the nonimage areas were wholly hydrated. The dehydrated fibrils faintly reflect a yellowish light, which accounts for the image. The scientists noted that the entire Shroud is very gradually yellowing with age, which means that eventually the image will no longer be visible.

Blood was chemically removed from some bloodstained fibrils. Although these fibrils came from areas where one would expect an image, there was no yellowing of the fibrils under the blood. In other words, where there are bloodstains, there is no image. This indicates that the blood was transferred to the Shroud first and the image sometime later.

It was also found, from the fibrils, that where one fiber crossed over another, there was a white spot on the underlying one. This indicates that the top fibril protected the underlying one from the image-making process.

TRANSFER OF THE IMAGE
FROM BODY TO CLOTH

The conclusion of the scientists is that the image is a scorch that is slightly different from the known scorches (from the fire in 1532), but nevertheless a true scorch. Not all of the scientists were prepared to say definitely that the image is a scorch, because no one could come up with a "technologically credible image transfer mechanism." In other words, bodies in a state of rigor mortis have not been known to emit heat, light, laser beams, or any other type of rays that are capable of scorching cloth.

FLASH PHOTOLYSIS

In scientific terms, it was concluded that the Shroud image is the result of yellowish cellulose fibrils that were changed to that color by some dehydration process caused by an extremely brief burst of radiant energy or, to be more technical, "by flash photolysis." This phenomenon was seen in Hiroshima after the dropping of the atom bomb. The flash of the explosion discolored concrete to a light reddish tint, leaving permanent shadows of a large valve, a gas-pump handle, rectangular towers, and other objects on the concrete.

Science, at this point in time, is not in a position to say what caused the burst of energy nor what type of energy resulted in the Shroud's being scorched. The New Testament is of little help in this regard, although Matthew does hint at some type of brilliant light displayed around Christ's tomb and the other Gospel writers make similar references: "Now afer the Sabbath, toward the dawn of the first day of the week, Mary Magdalene and the other Mary went to see the sepulchre. And behold there was a great earthquake; for an angel of the Lord descended from heaven and came and rolled back the stone and sat upon it. His appearance was like lightning and his raiment was as snow."*

OTHER HYPOTHESES
CONCERNING THE IMAGE

Scientists have tested other hypotheses regarding the formation of the image, but all were rejected for various reasons. STURP determined that the image of the Shroud is superficial (i.e., only the top fibrils of the cloth's fibers were affected), detailed, thermally stable, directionless, chemically stable, water stable, lacking in pigments, and has encoded three-dimensional information. These criteria seem to rule out the possibility that the image was created by some sort of painting.

Others have suggested that the image could have been created by a medieval or ancient artist using a hot metal statue with linen pressed on it. This was tried by the STURP scientists, but the resulting scorched image failed the three-dimensional test. The VP-8 Analyzer indicated curvature, but not distance, as the Shroud image does. The image from the hot metal statue was also grossly distorted when run through the VP-8 Analyzer. Joe Nickel, in his book, *Inquest on the Shroud of Turin,* stated that a monochromatic rubbing on cloth with powder over a bas-relief produces an image similar to that on the Shroud. Such an image, however, would fail both the three-dimensional and superfi-

*Matthew 28:1–3.

ciality tests. Rubbings result in a faint image on the reverse side of the paper or cloth. There is no image on the reverse side of the shroud. Although a medieval artist might, in some way, be able to create a credible image with a "hot statue" or "rubbing" technique, he still would need to include the bloodstains, presumably by painting with pigments or blood. The bloodstains would have to be added to the Shroud before the image was created. The Shroud includes both arterial and venous bloodstains from the flogging, beating, and crowning; from the premortem flows (nailing to the cross); and from the postmortem flows (wound in the side) before removal from the cross and blood from the postburial flows while the corpse was lying in the tomb. Many pathologists in the twentieth century have attested to the accuracy of all bloodstains on the Shroud based on the assumption that the man of the Shroud is Jesus or someone else crucified in the same way. It would seem impossible for anyone to paint with pigments or blood the marks of the crucifixion of Jesus in such a manner that it would not be apparent to a modern-day pathologist.

It is probably safe, therefore, to conclude that, if the Shroud of Turin is a hoax, it was not created by painting, a hot-statue scorch, or "rubbing." No one as yet has been able to propose a viable way for someone to produce the Shroud of Turin without crucifying a man in the same way as Jesus and wrapping him in an ancient linen cloth produced in the Near East with pollen grains from the area around Jerusalem, southern Turkey, and Constantinople. The perpetrator of any hoax would also have to produce the image in some manner that modern scientists cannot yet define and remove the body from the cloth without smearing the bloodstains. The chances of this having occurred must be infinitesimal.

For those who wish to explore the other scientific findings in regard to image formation, the book *Verdict on the Shroud*, by Stevenson and Habermas, is suggested.

CONCLUSIONS

It would seem that all of the evidence accumulated to date concerning the image indicates that one of two general conclusions can be reached:

1. The image is a light scorch caused by a natural process that has not yet been scientifically determined.
2. The image is a light scorch caused by supernatural events that humanity may never be able to explain completely in scientific terms.

Some other important conclusions that may be drawn from the bloodstains and the body image are:

1. The man depicted on the Shroud was a Jew, crucified by the Romans, and buried, for the most part, in accordance with ancient Jewish burial customs.
2. The blood was transferred onto the Shroud before the image was transmitted to the cloth.
3. The man was dead when the image was formed.
4. There is substantial agreement between the accounts of Jesus' crucifixion and burial as recorded in the New Testament and the logical conclusions from the scientific findings in regard to the image on the Shroud.

Part 6
Pollen on the Shroud

Ian Wilson, a British historian, was the first author to trace the history of the Shroud from Jerusalem to Turin. In his book, *The Shroud of Turin*, he identifies Jerusalem, Edessa (now Urfa), Constantinople (now Istanbul), France, and Italy as the places where the Shroud resided for prolonged periods of time.

As mentioned previously, Dr. Max Frei, the retired head of the Zurich Police Scientific Laboratory, viewed the Shroud at close range in 1973. He has an international reputation for analysis of microscopic substances. Frei noticed that the Shroud was covered with minute dust particles. He was given permission to remove some of these particles, which he did by means of sticky tape, covering twelve locations on the cloth. What Frei did was press small pieces of clear tape onto the Shroud, which were then removed and placed in individual envelopes. He analyzed the particles left on the tapes by using optic and electron microscopes. He found, among other types of debris, many species of pollen grains from flowering plants that had accumulated on the cloth over the centuries. Frei photographed the pollen through a microscope and matched them to their originating plants by reference to files of known varieties. Each genus of seed-bearing plants produces different-appearing pollen, whose characteristics last for thousands of years. Some of these pollen grains are smooth, others fuzzy, some spherical, some grooved, and so on. Pollen can be carried hundreds of miles by air currents. Frei found that the large volume and spectrum of pollens from Palestine, Turkey, and Western Europe could not be explained by storms or accidental contamination. Experiments have shown that 95 percent of the pollen collected from an object is grown within an area of a few hundred meters. Frei, therefore, was convinced that the Shroud had been in Palestine, Turkey, and Western Europe during some periods in its history.

In all, he found the pollen from forty-nine varieties of plants, of which thirty-eight grew in the Holy Land. The following thirteen plants are of particular interest because of their growth in rather limited geographical areas, which include Palestine:

SPECIES	GEOGRAPHICAL AREA
ANABIS APHYLLA	A desert plant found in southern Palestine, southeast Iran, Arabia, Crimea, and Morocco.
ACACIA ALBIDA	A desert plant very common in the Jordan Valley and around the Dead Sea.
ARTEMISIA HERBA-ALBA	Semidesert plant particularly prevalent east of Jerusalem but also in other areas where the ground has a high salt content.
ECHINOPS GLABERRIMUS	A North African plant found in rocky areas.
FAGONIA MOLLIS	A desert plant frequently found in the Jordan Valley, but also found in the Sahara Desert and Arabia.
HALOXILON PERSICUM	A desert plant found in Palestine, Turkistan and Iran.
HELIANTHEMUM VESICARIUM	A plant native to the steppes and rocky semidesert regions from Iran to Morocco.
HYOSCYAMUS AUREUS	A cliff plant found on old walls and ruins. Found in Eastern Mediterranean, Iran, and Turkistan regions.
OLIGOMERIS SUBULATA	A desert plant that grows in sand and limestone from Iran to Morocco.

ONOSMA ORIENTALIS	A cliff plant found on old walls and ruins in Palestine, Iran, Iraq, Syria, Turkey, and Lebanon.
SUAEDA AEGYPTICA	A desert plant found in the Sahara Desert and Arabia.
TAMARIX NILOTICA	A desert bush found in the Sahara Desert and Arabia.
ZYGOPHYLLUM DUMOSUM	A bush most frequently found in the desert around the Dead Sea.

Jerusalem is about fifteen miles west of the Dead Sea and the river Jordan. The pollen from desert plants, therefore, probably fills the air in Jerusalem when the wind is from the east. Three of the above plants—*Artemisia, Suaeda,* and *Tamarix*—are particularly useful in diagnosing plant life near Jerusalem because they are halophytes, i.e., plants adapted to soil with a high salt content. The ground around the Dead Sea is, of course, full of sodium chloride.

Frei also found that the Shroud was probably in all of the other primary areas indicated by Wilson in his history of the cloth. For instance, Frei found pollen from nineteen species of plants, which confirmed that Edessa or its environs had been a place of residence for the Shroud. He likewise, found fourteen species from Constantinople, thirteen from France, and sixteen from Italy. Some plants are found in more than one of the above locations. Almost all of the plants growing in France were found to be also growing in Italy. There was also some plant overlap between Jerusalem and Edessa.

Dr. Frei is convinced that the pollen evidence proves that the Shroud was at one time in Palestine. He also publically affirmed that the Shroud was in the Anatolian steppe area (near the modern towns of Urfa, Bitlis Diyarbakir, Mardin, Gazeantep, and Malatya in southern Turkey, adjacent to the Syrian border). Urfa is, of course, the modern name of Edessa, where Ian Wilson states the Shroud was located for some 900 years after leaving Jerusalem. Wilson, in his book, marshals considerable evidence that the so-called Mandylion of Edessa was the same piece of cloth as the Shroud of Turin. Max Frei agrees with this theory of the Mandylion/Shroud. It is very important, therefore, when considering the history of the Shroud, to have the independent scientific evidence that indicates that the Shroud, in all probability was, at some period in time, located in Edessa. The pollen evidence also supports Wilson's contentions that besides Edessa, the Shroud was in Constantinople, France, and Italy.

The pollen analysis fits in nicely with the other pieces of the puzzle. It was previously concluded (in part 3) that the Shroud was a primitive piece of linen woven in the Near East. The New Testament states that Jesus was buried in a linen cloth in this area:

> . . . for the place where Jesus was crucified was near the city [Jerusalem]. . . .
>
> —John 19:20

> They took the body of Jesus and bound it in linen cloths with the spices, as is the burial custom of the Jews. Now in the place where He was crucified, there was a garden and in the garden a new tomb where no one had ever been laid. So because of the Jewish day of Preparation, as the tomb was close at hand, they laid Jesus there.
>
> —John 19:41–42

The pollen analysis indicates that the Shroud most certainly was in the Near East, particularly Palestine, which ties in with the Gospel account of the burial of Jesus.

Part 7
Jerusalem to Edessa

The scientific findings in regard to the Shroud repeatedly lead back to the New Testament accounts of the crucifixion and burial of Jesus Christ. Particularly noteworthy are the wounds of the Shroud figure as compared with those reported in the Gospels, such as: the injuries to the wrists and feet, a gaping hole between the fifth and sixth ribs, the marks of lacerations from a severe scourging, a bruised face, further puncture wounds around the head, and a right shoulder that had been rubbed raw. The damaged knee, the expanded chest cavity, the bent hands and feet, which are stiffened into unnatural positions in rigor mortis, also appear to relate to the Gospel accounts. The findings in regard to the cloth as a textile indicate that it could have been available at the time of the crucifixion, and the pollen analysis fixes Jerusalem as a place where the cloth resided at some time during its history. Other findings indicate that the man depicted on the Shroud was a Jew or Arab, crucified by the Romans. In other words, all of the pieces of the puzzle seem to fit together and they strongly indicate that the image is of Jesus. Robert Bucklin, a clinical pathologist and professor at the University of California, who researched the Shroud for some thirty years, has stated: "If I were asked in a court of law to stake my professional reputation on the validity of the Shroud of Turin, I would answer very positively and firmly that it's the burial cloth of Christ—and that it is Jesus whose figure appears on the Shroud." Later he added: "It's not a matter of faith to me; it's just a matter of common sense." *

In complex matters, science of course, deals in probabilities. For example, theories such as those of the origin of the species, relativity, the big-bang origin of the universe, and others are not claimed to be absolute truths, but are merely the best explanations that fit the proven facts. When new facts are uncovered, former theories are often modified or discarded. No one can say with 100 percent certainty that the image on the Shroud is that of Jesus, but it does seem that the probability is very high. Assuming that it is Jesus, the Gospels are able to provide the initial history of the Shroud:

And he [Joseph of Arimathea] brought a linen shroud, and taking Him [Jesus] down [from the cross], wrapped Him in the linen shroud, and laid Him in a tomb which had been hewn out of the rock; and he rolled a stone against the door of the tomb.
—Mark 15:46

Now on the first day of the week Mary Magdalene came to the tomb early, while it was still dark, and saw that the stone had been taken away from the tomb.
—John 20:1

Then Simon Peter came following him [another disciple] and went into the tomb; he saw the linen cloths lying, and the napkin, which had been on His head, not lying with the linen cloths but rolled up in a place by itself.
—John 20:6–8

After this, there are no further references in the New Testament to linen cloths or a shroud. One other ancient source, the apocryphal gospel of the Hebrews, however, states that after the resurrection: "Now the Lord, when he had given the linen cloth to the servant of the priest [probably Peter] went to James and appeared to him. . . ."

*National Review, April 16, 1982, p. 416. Reprinted with permission from National Review Inc., 150 East 35th Street, New York, N.Y. 10016.

At this time, circa A.D. 33, it might be assumed that Peter (or some other disciple) had the Shroud in Jerusalem or its vicinity. If this was the case, it seems strange that there is no mention of a shroud with an imprinted image in the Gospels. When one considers the customs of the Jews of this period, however, it is perhaps not so strange. In the first place, anything that touched a corpse was considered unclean and anyone who came in contact with such an object was required to go through a ritual of purification. If the Shroud fell into the hands of the religious authorities, it would most certainly have been burned. The religious Jews of this period also took the second commandment very seriously and assumed that pictures, as images to worship, were not to be tolerated: "You shall not make for yourself a graven image or any likeness of anything that is in heaven above or that is in the earth beneath or that is in the water under the earth." In addition, any potential Jewish converts to Christianity in that period would, in all probability, be horrified and repelled by an image on a grave cloth of a nude man who had suffered the most ignominious of all executions, usually reserved for the worst types of criminals, slaves, or enemies of the state. The Christian leaders, therefore, were probably torn between disposing of the Shroud according to custom (i.e., by burning) or preserving this record of Christ's last days on earth, but keeping it under cover. The apostles obviously chose the later course of action.

Our semilegendary story now shifts to Edessa (a city then outside the Roman empire), located north of Jerusalem, about forty miles beyond the current Syrian border in southeastern Turkey. In the first century A.D., Edessa was the capital of a principality called Mesopotamia, which was aligned with the Parthian Empire to the east. Edessa, an important city at that time, was ruled by Abgar V between A.D. 13 and 50. Abgar suffered from some incurable disease, probably leprosy. Having heard of the healing miracles of Jesus, the king sent a messenger to Jerusalem, asking Jesus to come to Edessa or, if he couldn't come, to send a likeness of himself. Jesus, however, had departed this world by the time the messenger arrived in Jerusalem. The church fathers, after hearing the message, decided that this would be a good opportunity to send the Shroud to a safer place than Palestine. Abgar, a pagan and used to images, would not only find a picture of Jesus acceptable, but also might consider it a means for effecting a cure. Meanwhile, the Shroud would be safe from the Jewish religious authorities in Jerusalem. Nevertheless, it did not seem appropriate to send a reigning monarch a grave cloth, particularly one with the gruesome record of a brutal crucifixion. It was decided, therefore, to change the Shroud into a facial portrait by folding the cloth into eighths, in such a way that only the face was visible. The folded Shroud was then placed in a rectangular box with a circular opening through which it was possible to view only the face. The box was later covered with golden trelliswork, in a design that was commonly used to embellish the headdresses and robes of Parthian nobles and kings by an Edessian named Aggai, who was famous for this type of work. Because the image was not centered on the Shroud, the three-inch side piece is thought to have been added at this time (sometime between A.D. 33 and 50).

Now that the Shroud was suitably framed, another problem arose—namely, the bloodstains on the face from the cap of thorns. It was believed that it would be better to claim that this was a picture of the living Christ rather than a death mask. Abgar, therefore, was told that these markings were caused by the bloody sweat in the Garden of Gethsemane, as recorded in Luke: "And being in an agony He prayed more earnestly; and His sweat became like great drops of blood falling down upon the ground." * According to legend, Jesus pressed a towel to his face in the garden and his image was imprinted on the cloth.

The portrait, in its golden frame, was entrusted to Thaddæus an early convert to Christianity, who took it to Edessa. An ancient account of what happened next in Abgar's throne room follows:

> [Thaddæus] placed it on his forehead like a sign. Abgar saw his coming from a distance, and thought he saw a light shining from his face which no eye could stand, which the portrait Thadd-

*Luke 22:45.

69

æus was wearing produced. Abgar was dumbfounded by the unbearable glow of the brightness, and, as though forgetting the ailments he had and the long paralysis of his legs, he at once got up from his bed and compelled himself to run. In making his paralyzed limbs go to meet Thaddæus, he felt the same feeling, though in a different way, as those who saw that face flashing with lightning on Mount Tabor. And so receiving the likeness from the apostle . . . immediately he felt the leprosy cleansed and gone. Having been instructed then by the apostle more clearly of the doctrine of truth . . . he asked about the likeness portrayed on the linen cloth. For when he had carefully inspected it he saw that it did not consist of earthly colors, and he was astonished at its power. . . . At this Thaddæus explained about the time of the agony and that the likeness was due to sweat, not pigments. . . . *

There are in existence a number of ancient accounts of this event which have been incorporated into the beliefs of the Eastern Orthodox Church as the Doctrine of Addai (Thaddæus is Greek for "Addai" in the old Syriac language.)

Ian Wilson, believes that because there are so many ancient documents that describe the Abgar event, it must have a basis in fact. Although there is not complete agreement between the various versions, Wilson seemingly has done a good job of separating fact from legend in regard to the Doctrine of Addai.

King Abgar V is shown receiving the image of Jesus' face from Thaddæus in a painting in Saint Catherine's Monastery. The face image is matted to provide a distinct horizontal format. This Orthodox monastery was built at the bottom of Mount Sinai by the emperor Justinian the Great (circa A.D. 540).

Thaddæus remained in Edessa, where he also cured a man, Abdu, described as The Second Man of the Kingdom. Thaddæus preached a sermon and continued to win Edessian converts from paganism, including Aggai, the designer of golden trelliswork.

A primitive Christian church became established to a degree in Edessa during the reign of Abgar V and his son who succeeded him on the throne. Circa A.D. 57, however, a second son of Abgar

*As quoted by Ian Wilson in *The Shroud of Turin*, rev. ed. (Garden City, N.Y.: Doubleday, 1979), p. 129.

V succeeded to the throne, and he made the city revert to paganism. He persecuted the Christians who hid the Shroud (or the Mandylion, as it was later called in Edessa) in a niche above the west gate of the city. The Shroud/Mandylion was preserved in its niche, which was blocked up with bricks for almost 500 years. When the Gospels were being written, circa A.D. 70–100, the Shroud, with its image, was safely walled up and out of sight in distant Edessa. During its stay in Jerusalem, it had been carefully hidden because of its being an anathema to religious Jews. It is not too surprising, therefore, that the evangelists were either unaware of its existence, or were confused about its true nature, because there is no mention of it in their New Testament writings.

Christianity was reintroduced in Edessa around A.D. 177, but the memory of the Mandylion (the Shroud in its golden frame) had become dim and its location unknown to many while it remained under tightly sealed conditions above the west gate of the city.

In the early years of the fourth century A.D., the Roman emperor Constantine became a Christian and made Christianity the official religion of the empire. He moved the capital from Rome to Byzantium, which, in A.D. 330, he renamed Constantinople. He also attempted to make the new capital the religious as well as the political center of the empire. His mother, Saint Helena, began the collection of Christian relics from Palestine and elsewhere that, of course, was sent to Constantinople and placed in the charge of the Ecumenical Patriarch, who served as an eastern counterpart to the Pope in Rome.

By the year A.D. 525, Edessa had become a part of the Eastern Roman or Byzantine Empire. Rome had fallen to the Visigoths, and the western part of the old Roman Empire had been split up among the invading Germanic tribes, although the Pope exercised political authority in and around Rome. In that year, Edessa suffered severe flooding from the Daisan River that killed some 30,000 people, destroyed many buildings, and weakened the walls of the city. At this time, the niche was broken open and the Shroud/Mandylion rediscovered. The cloth was identified as the original portrait that had been brought to Abgar V. It was considered to be the image of Christ. Acheiropoietos—Greek for "Not Made by Human Hands." The Byzantine emperor Justinian aided in the reconstruction of the city of Edessa, which included building a large cathedral, the Hagia Sophia in Edessa, to house the cloth, which was regarded as being so holy that it was rarely displayed in public, except at a time of crisis such as a siege of the city. From this time onward, Christ began to be depicted in art in a number of new ways that can definitely be traced to the Shroud image.

There is no doubt, from the many historical accounts and Frei's pollen analysis, that the Mandylion was in Edessa for many years, both before and after its rediscovery. It has also been referred to as the Napkin of Jesus and the Holy Image of Edessa. What Ian Wilson has established, however, is that the Mandylion is in fact the same piece of linen as the Holy Shroud of Turin. This was accomplished by research into the history of art, which will be described in part 8 of this volume.

Part 8
The Image and Art

Paul Vignon, an art historian as well as a biologist, was the first to note, in 1902, that many paintings, frescoes, mosaics, tapestries, and icons of Christ included markings similar to those found on the facial image of the Shroud. No pictures of Jesus are known to have been made during his lifetime. There also are no descriptions of Jesus' appearance in the New Testament. Saint Augustine wrote in the fifth century: "We know not his earthly appearance, nor that of his mother."

EARLY PICTURES OF JESUS

Christians began to create images of Jesus as early as the third century A.D. and perhaps earlier, particularly in the catacombs of Rome. The early artists did not know what Jesus looked like, and consequently there was considerable variation in his appearance from artist to artist.

Artists, therefore, rendered Jesus in many ways, particularly until the middle of the sixth century. They usually depicted Christ as an innocent-looking, young, beardless man with short hair. (See Illustration 11.) These early renderings were generally dissimilar to one another and often looked more like the pagan god Apollo than a bearded Jew.

Illustration 11 shows Jesus as a young, beardless man with short hair. Although this mosaic was produced a few years after the rediscovery of the Mandylion/Shroud in Edessa, it is typical of the early renderings of Christ before art began to be influenced by the Shroud image. This mosaic of Jesus with the archangels can be found in the apse of Saint Vitale, in Ravenna, Italy.

Other Apollo-like renderings of Jesus produced prior to the sixth century.

SIXTH-CENTURY AND LATER RENDITIONS
OF JESUS

A few years after A.D. 525, the year in which the Mandylion/Shroud was rediscovered, Jesus began to be pictured as a mature, Semitic-looking man with long hair, a full, forked beard, a long nose, and deep-set eyes with large pupils. The whole countenance is usually set in a rigid posture and faces front. It was also noted that the renditions began to resemble one another, although some artists, then as now, may have merely copied the works of others. These changes in the way Christ was depicted occurred particularly in Byzantine art, although the same tendencies can be found in art produced in western Europe. Paul Vignon noted these changes particularly because of his interest in the similarities between the image on the Shroud and many of the paintings, mosaics, and other artworks produced in the latter part of the sixth century and later. It is well known that artists visited Edessa to view the Mandylion, with some coming from as far as 1,000 miles away.

VIGNON'S SCIENTIFIC APPROACH TO ART

Vignon, with his scientific training, attempted to find specific similarities between the Shroud image and works of art, as clues to the possible existence of the Shroud prior to the fourteenth century. He found many similarities between the Shroud and works of art, of which a few did not make pictorial sense, i.e., they arose from such sources as creases in the cloth or imperfections in the weave. In total, Vignon listed twenty markings, of which fifteen are generally accepted as being quite obvious (the others being questionable). The fifteen Vignon markings are:

1. A transverse streak across the forehead.
2. A rectangle with one side missing on the forehead.

3. A v shape at the bridge of the nose.
4. A second v shape within the rectangle with one side missing (2 above).
5. A raised right eyebrow.
6. An accentuated left cheek.
7. An accentuated right cheek.
8. An enlarged left nostril.
9. An accentuated line between nose and upper lip.
10. A heavy line under lower lip.
11. A hairless area between lip and beard.
12. A forked beard.
13. A transverse line across the throat.
14. Heavily accentuated, owlish eyes.
15. Loose strands of hair falling from the apex of the forehead.

These features were incorporated in many works of art beginning in the sixth century, but not before. All of these markings were not included in all works of art, but their persistent appearance makes it appear as though many artists were working from a common blueprint.

ART FROM A COMMON BLUEPRINT

The well-known eleventh-century mosaic of Christ Pantocrator in the dome of the monastery church in Daphni near Athens, Greece, includes thirteen of the fifteen Vignon markings. (See Illustration 12.) Two early (sixth-century) examples are the mosaic of Christ enthroned, in the Sant'Apollinare Nuovo Church in Ravenna, Italy (which includes eight Vignon markings, as shown in Illustration 13), and a medallion portrait on a silver vase from Syria. There is an eighth-century example in a painting in the catacomb of Saint Pontianus in Rome that has eight Vignon markings. In the South Gallery of the Hagia Sophia, Constantinople, there is a thirteenth-century mosaic of Christ enthroned with eleven Vignon markings. (See Illustration 14.) There is also another mosaic of Christ with Vignon markings in the South Gallery of the Hagia Sophia. (See Illustration 15.)

Illustration 12 shows Jesus as a Semitic-looking man with long hair, a full forked beard, a long nose, and deep-set eyes with large pupils. This rendering was in all probability influenced by the Shroud image. Note the similarities between this image and Illustrations 13 through 19.

Mosaic of Christ, with Eight Vignon Markings

Illustration 13 is one of the earliest pictures of Jesus based on the Mandylion/Shroud, rediscovered in A.D. 525. It was produced only a few years after Illustration 11, but note the great difference in the appearance of Jesus. This mosaic is located in the Saint Apollinare Nuovo Church, in Ravenna.

Mosaic of Christ, with Eleven Vignon Markings

Illustration 14 shows Jesus enthroned between the emperor Constantine and the empress Zoe. It is in the South Gallery of the Hagia Sophia, in Constantinople.

Mosaic of Christ, with Eight Vignon Markings

Illustration 15 is another mosaic from the Hagia Sophia, in Constantinople, showing Vignon markings.

One of the finest examples of a mosaic with fifteen Vignon markings can be found in the apse of the Norman-Byzantine church in Cefalu, Sicily. (See Illustration 16.) It dates back to the twelfth century A.D. There are many other examples of images of Christ with Vignon markings.

Some artists have used one or perhaps several Vignon markings when depicting a saint or other holy person. An example of this can be seen in Illustration 17, a twentieth-century painting by Georges Rouault, who titled it *Holy Face*. The history of art has indicated that the Shroud has been in existence at least since the sixth century A.D. because otherwise there is no known explanation for the large amount of artwork traceable to the Shroud/Mandylion beginning in the mid–sixth century but not before. The Shroud, of course, was sealed in an Edessan wall from circa A.D. 60 until A.D. 525.

THE POWER OF THE MANDYLION/SHROUD

In A.D. 544, the Persians laid seige to Edessa. The Mandylion was brought out to aid the Edessans in repulsing the enemy. Because the Edessans were successful, many of the surrounding towns wanted copies that had been in contact with the Mandylion and had thereby acquired miraculous powers, according to common belief. Edward Gibbon, in his *Decline and Fall of the Roman Empire,* wrote: "Before the end of the sixth century, these images made without hands were propagated in the camps and cities of the Eastern Empire; they were the objects of worship and the instruments of miracles, and in the hour of danger or tumult their venerable presence could revive the hope, rekindle the courage, or repress the fury of the Roman legions." *

There are no known copies of the Mandylion from the Edessan period that have survived, but some copies made in the tenth century, after the transfer of the cloth to Constantinople (A.D. 944), and later are still extant. An early–tenth-century

*Edward Gibbon, *Decline and Fall of the Roman Empire,* vol. 3 (New York, N.Y.: Heritage Press, 1946), p. 1672.

Mosaic of Christ, with Fifteen Vignon Markings

Illustration 16 shows a twelfth-century mosaic of Christ Pantocrator. It is located in the cathedral in Cefalu, Sicily.

Holy Face, by Georges Rouault

Illustration 17 shows Vignon markings in *Holy Face,* by Georges Rouault.

fresco (now destroyed) of the Mandylion was located in Spas Nereditsa, Russia. It included nine of the fifteen Vignon markings. (See Illustration 18.) The head was in a circular area, and surrounding the circular area was trelliswork similar to that used to embellish the headdress of Parthian kings (probably copied from the golden box). The Eastern Orthodox church continues to make copies of the Mandylion. Illustration 19 is an early–sixteenth-century painting on cloth, an icon labeled *Acheiropoietos,* meaning the original was "not made by human hands." The Russian branch of orthodoxy provided cloth copies of the Mandylion that were used as battle standards as late as World War I. Under the Marxist-Leninist government, this practice is not sanctioned. Many of these standards are labeled "Acheiropoietos." There is a picture of World War I Russian troops with a Mandylion flag in the Imperial War Museum, in London. The face of Christ is in the middle, and around it is depicted a frame of trelliswork. A Mandylion was also used as a battle standard by Ivan the Terrible, as can be seen in the Museum of Arms, in Moscow.

The Mandylion tradition lives on in the Orthodox church, although the Mandylion itself passed from history in 1204, when Constantinople was sacked by the armies of the Fourth Crusade. Prior to the sack of Constantinople, the Byzantines removed the Shroud from its golden box or frame, and thereby the Mandylion became again the Shroud that we know today. When the unpinning occurred, in the late tenth or early eleventh century, the Doctrine of Addai and the Mandylion tradition were well established in Eastern Orthodoxy. The church authorities probably retained the golden box and did not choose to explain that what had been believed for centuries, i.e., that the cloth contained only a face image, needed to be updated. The Shroud was put back into its Mandylion box from time to time for display purposes, but after the sack of Constantinople in 1204, the golden box was not heard of again. Nevertheless, the Byzantines rigidly maintained the old Abgar story in both art and literature. Scenes of the Mandylion's history incorporated in icons produced in more modern times always end with the tenth century, when the cloth came to Constantinople.

Fresco of the Mandylion with Nine Vignon Markings

Illustration 18 is the earliest extant picture of the Mandylion/Shroud image. The design outside the circle is thought to be a representation of the golden trelliswork on the box that encased the Shroud during much of its first thousand years of existence Illustration from THE SHROUD OF TURIN by Ian Wilson, Copyright © 1978 by Ian Wilson. Reprinted by permission of Doubleday & Company, Inc.

Illustration 19 is one of many representations of the Mandylion. This one was painted in the sixteenth century. It is called the Vernicle, although that term is usually reserved for Veronica's Veil. Many of the Vignon markings have been retained, but the trelliswork observable in Illustration 18 has been considerably modified.

VERONICA'S VEIL—ANOTHER IMAGE
NOT MADE BY HANDS

When the tradition of an image of Christ's face being impressed on a cloth is considered, the legend of Veronica's Veil may very well come to mind. This story, in an uncomplicated version, was told by a French priest, Adrien Parvillieps, S.J., in the seventeenth century:

> Veronica was in her house when she heard the shouting and wailing from a crowd surrounding the soldiers who were leading Jesus to Calvary. She rose hurriedly, put her head to the door, looked over the heads of the crowd, and saw our Redeemer. . . . Transported, beside herself, she seized her veil and threw herself into the street, oblivious to the insults and blows from the soldiers who pushed her back. Arriving in the presence of our Savior, whose face was pouring with sweat and blood, she wiped [his face] with her veil. . . . All honor to you, courageous woman. . . . The Savior granted you the most precious gift which he could make to a creature of this world, his portrait imprinted . . . on your veil.*

This story became widespread in the Middle Ages. It is represented today as the sixth station of the cross in most Roman Catholic churches. The basic story as recorded above is simple and appealing, but there are other more complex and conflicting legends about Veronica, some of which go back to at least the fourth century A.D. Ian Wilson gave up attempting to separate fact from legend in the stories of Veronica. There is, however, a relationship between the Veil and the Shroud of Turin.

In A.D. 1011, a cloth copy of the Mandylion was sent to Rome from Constantinople. It was called the "vera ikon" (Latin for "true likeness") by the Byzantines. In Rome, "vera ikon" was interpreted to mean Veronica. Pope Sergius therefore consecrated an altar in a chapel in the old Saint Peter's Basilica to what was believed to be the Veronica relic. In the 1190s, someone

---

*Ian Wilson, *The Shroud of Turin*, rev. ed. (Garden City, N.Y.: Doubleday, 1979), p. 106.

in Constantinople sent the Pope an ornamental tapestry canopy to be held over the "Veronica" when it was displayed. The centerpiece depicted a representation of Christ in exactly the same manner as can be seen on the Shroud. This would seem to indicate that the Veil might have come from the Shroud. History records that the "Veronica Veil" was last heard of in A.D. 1527, when Charles V sacked Rome. The Veil was one of several relics seized by soldiers, who later attempted to sell it in the taverns of Rome. Medieval artists, however, continued to find Veronica's Veil a popular subject for years after the original passed from the scene.

SUMMATION

Research into the history of art has made it possible to trace the Shroud back almost to its inception. History does not record when King Abgar requested the presence of Jesus or his picture, but the king died in A.D. 50. The establishment of primitive Christianity in Edessa during Abgar's reign is a well-documented fact, as is the rediscovery of the Mandylion in Edessa after the disastrous flood of A.D. 525. A study of art produced after the Mandylion reappeared in the sixth century strongly indicates that the Shroud and the Mandylion are the same piece of cloth. As mentioned earlier, the pollen analysis indicates that the Shroud was in Edessa during a substantial period of time, which gives support to the Mandylion/Shroud theory. Furthermore, the history of art indicates that the idea of an image of Jesus' face imprinted on a cloth and "not made with human hands" can be traced back to the Shroud of Turin, which spawned first the Mandylion and from it the Veil of Veronica. Many other paintings, frescoes, mosaics, and similar works of art can be traced to the Shroud by means of the Vignon markings.

Part 9
Edessa to Constantinople

As previously mentioned, much of Edessa was destroyed in the flood of A.D. 525. The Shroud/Mandylion, however, in its niche in the wall above the west gate, was not harmed. The Edessans soon discovered the Shroud/Mandylion in its hiding place after the flood had undermined and cracked open the niche in the wall. The Shroud/Mandylion was almost immediately recognized as the "true likeness" of Christ that had been sent to Abgar. (The Doctrine of Addai had survived the intervening centuries.)

As this period in its history, Edessa was a part of the Byzantine Empire. The emperor, Justinian, therefore, aided the Edessans in providing flood control and rebuilding the city. He also built for them the Hagia Sophia, as he had built the Hagia Sophia in Constantinople. The Shroud/Mandylion, still in its box with the golden trelliswork, was then placed in the Saint Sophia Cathedral (the Hagia Sophia). The general public, however, had little access to the cloth, but artists and others, who traveled up to 1,000 miles to view it, apparently were allowed to see the image of the face through the circular hole in the golden box. This had a profound influence on Christian art, as was related in part 8.

During these years, Edessa became an increasingly important center of Eastern Orthodox Christianity. History records that at one point, there were more than 300 Christian churches and monasteries in and around Edessa. In the caves near the city lived thousands of hermits and monks. In A.D. 638, the

Muslim Arabs conquered Edessa, but they allowed Christianity to continue. The Arabs admired and helped preserve the Hagia Sophia, which housed the Mandylion. In the twelfth century, however, the Muslim Turks gained control and persecuted the Christians to the point where today there is no operating Christian church in Urfa, as the city was renamed in the fifteenth century.

The Shroud might have been destroyed during the period of Iconoclasm when in both the Byzantine and Muslim empires, many icons and other manmade images were demolished. The Shroud/Mandylion, however, came through this period (A.D. 723–842) unscathed, perhaps because it was considered to be "not made with human hands."

Around A.D. 940, the Byzantine emperor Romanus I (Lecapenus) reached his seventieth year and, reflecting on his long reign, decided that in order to quiet his troubled conscience, he should do something to strengthen the Christian faith. By that time, it was evident that the Iconoclasts had lost the day. His empire again abounded with religious art, but the greatest of all images lay hundreds of miles away, in Edessa, which was then in Muslim territory. The emperor felt that it would be a fitting climax to his reign if he could move the Mandylion to his capital, Constantinople. The emperor, therefore, sent an army to Edessa in early 943 with the sole purpose of obtaining this relic. On its way there, some 200 Muslims were taken hostage by the Byzantine army. Edessa was placed under siege, but the commanding general agreed to spare the city if the Mandylion was surrendered to a Bishop Abraham, who represented the emperor. In addition, the army would free the 200 hostages and pay 12,000 pieces of silver. This offer was forwarded to Baghdad, the Muslim capital at that time, by the emir of Edessa. There the caliph decided that the cloth should be turned over to the invading army. This decision was finally made, based largely on the desire to free the hostages. The Christians of Edessa demonstrated vehemently against the surrender of the cloth, but it was eventually given to the invaders, in the early summer of 944. It is probably fortunate that the Shroud/Mandylion left Edessa at this time, well before the Turks took control of the city and destroyed the Hagia Sophia and the other historic churches.

On August 15, 944, the Shroud/Mandylion arrived in Constantinople, where the sons of the emperor found it "extremely blurred." The next day, in celebration of its arrival, it was carried about the walls of the city and into various churches and chapels. It was also placed on the emperor's throne of state and on the throne in the sanctuary of the Hagia Sophia in Constantinople. It was finally given a permanent place in the Chapel of the Pharos, where a large collection of the emperor's relics were kept. At this time, the Shroud was still pinned taut within the trellised golden box and no one realized that the cloth bore the images of a complete body.

The emperor Romanus I was forced to abdicate by his sons shortly after the arrival of the cloth in Constantinople. In January 945, the new emperor of the Byzantines caused a gold coin to be struck showing Christ enthroned, proclaimed August 16 as the Mandylion feast day in the Orthodox church calendar, and arranged for the writing of the history of the Mandylion, which was only recently translated into English at the request of Ian Wilson.

Sometime during the eleventh or twelfth century, the Shroud was unpinned and taken from its golden box. In 1177, a shroud was mentioned in the list of relics held by the emperor. In 1201, the keeper of the relics described the shroud as "of linen of cheap and easily obtainable material defying decay because it wrapped the mysterious, naked, dead body after the Passion." In 1204, Robert de Clari, a French author who accompanied the army of the Fourth Crusade, described the relics in Constantinople. He wrote about the Shroud as follows: ". . . there was another of the churches which they called My Lady St. Mary of Blachernae where was kept the Shroud in which our Lord had been wrapped, which stood up straight every Friday so that the figure of our Lord could be plainly seen there. . . . And no one either Greek or French even knew what became of this Shroud after the city was taken."

The Fourth Crusade was largely a French undertaking,

which ended in the army's sacking of Constantinople. (Originally the army merely planned to stop off in Constantinople on its way to the Holy Land, but when the military saw the wealth and splendor of the city it was decided to stay and plunder it.) The historian Edward Gibbon wrote:

> . . . . they trampled under foot the most venerable objects of Christian worship. In the Cathedral of Saint Sophia, the ample veil of the sanctuary was rent asunder for the sake of the golden fringe; and the altar, a monument of art and riches, was broken into pieces and shared among the captors. The mules and horses were laden with the wrought silver and gilt carvings which they tore from the doors and pulpit. . . . A prostitute was seated on the throne of the Patriarch and . . . sang and danced in the church to ridicule the hymns and processions of the Orientals.*

After the sack of Constantinople, the Mandylion was never seen again, but some 150 years later, the Shroud surfaced near Paris in the possession of a knight named Geoffrey de Charny. With financial help from the French king, he built a small wooden church in Lirey, a town near Paris, to house the Shroud. Neither he nor his family, relatively impecunious, revealed how they gained possession of this truly valuable relic. The loss of the Shroud/Mandylion, however, did not stop the process of copies being made of copies of the Mandylion in Greece, the Balkans, and Russia, up until and including modern times.

*Edward Gibbon, *Decline and Fall of the Roman Empire,* vol. 3 (New York, N.Y.: Heritage Press, 1946), p. 2134.

Part 10
Constantinople to Paris

After the sack of Constantinople (A.D. 1204) and until the Shroud of Turin was rediscovered in France in the 1350s, no one can be certain about the whereabouts of this relic. It would appear logical that a Frenchman from the crusading army brought it back to France, since many religious relics, both real and spurious, flooded France after the return of the crusaders from Constantinople. If this was the case, however, why was the valuable Shroud kept hidden for some 150 years, at a time when relics were very popular and expensive? There is a theory, but with little proof, that during these "missing" years, the Shroud was in the hands of the Knights Templar. This was a monastic order of knights dedicated to the defense of the Holy Land. It had been established some eighty years before the sack of Constantinople. In a short period of time, it had become wealthy and powerful, with a series of fortresses across Europe and the Near East. The Templars had become bankers, especially for kings and popes. They helped finance the Fourth Crusade. The Order of Knights Templar was a highly secret, religious, military organization with elaborate rituals and threats of death to those who revealed its mysteries. It is said that they had two thousand members in France alone and the largest treasury in Western Europe. Their international headquarters was in The Temple, a formidable fortress in Paris.

At the beginning of the fourteenth century, Europe was filled with rumors that the Templars were hiding and worshipping, as an idol, a mysterious head. This head was supposedly heavily bearded and had a fierce-looking face, about the size of that of a normal man. It was kissed, venerated, and called The Savior, according to the gossip of the day. As we know, from the Mandylion, when the Shroud is folded into eights, the image can be made to appear as only a disembodied head. The Templars were certainly in a position to have acquired the Shroud/Mandylion after the sack of Constantinople, and they may very well have made copies, since all of their temples appear to have had "heads," according to testimony taken during an inquisition. What is believed to be a copy was found in 1951 in Templecombe, England. Templecombe had at one time included a Knights Templar preceptory, which was used to recruit and train knights. During a severe gale, the ceiling plaster collapsed in a cottage outbuilding and revealed a panel painting covered with coal dust. Today the restored painting hangs in the tiny Church of Saint Mary, Templecombe. Judging its distinct medieval style, the painting could have been created by the Templars during this period. It conforms to the Templar descriptions from the inquisition as a painting on a plaque, a disembodied life-size head, with a grizzled, reddish beard. It also bears a striking resemblance to the Shroud/Mandylion pictures with some of the Vignon markings.

In 1307, the king of France, Philip the Fair, having exhausted all of his usual sources of revenue, decided to seize the treasury of the Knights Templar and at the same time break up this powerful organization that rivaled his own authority. The main charge was heresy. For this religious charge, he needed the assistance of the Pope, Clement V, who resided in Avignon, France. Clement was the first of the line of "French" Popes, which had been established in Avignon with the assistance of Philip the Fair. Although Clement was reluctant to authorize heresy trials of the Knights Templar, he was bullied by the king, to whom he was indebted, into conducting an inquisition, which often involved obtaining confessions by many types of torture.

The Pope, understandably, was not anxious to bring to trial the organization that had been "the sword arm of the Church in defense of the Holy Land," although the Templars had moved from their ideals of asceticism and poverty to great wealth and an international web of power, based, in no small part, on their banking activities. Their secret rituals added to their sinister reputation, which was enhanced by the current rumors of idol worship.

One night, in 1307, Philip the Fair seized the Paris Temple and arrested every Knights Templar in France. The treasury and the "head" that the knights supposedly worshipped could not be found. Shortly before the arrests, the grand master, Jacques de Molay, called for many of the Templar's books and rules and had them burned. An order was circulated to all French preceptories that no information regarding customs and rituals was to be released to anyone. There is evidence, therefore, that the Templars suspected or were tipped off that trouble was brewing. Five years later, the Pope abolished the order, not only in France but throughout Europe. It is interesting that no copies of the "head," which the Templars supposedly worshipped, were ever found, with the possible exception of the one in Temple-combe, England, that was discovered hundreds of years later, in 1951.

In France, the arrested Templars were imprisoned, tortured, and burned at the stake. Many strange accusations were made, and confessions were extracted under torture during the next seven years. Finally, in 1314 Jacques de Molay, the grand master, and Geoffrey de Charnay, the preceptor of Normandy, were brought out onto a scaffold in front of Notre Dame in Paris in order to repeat their "confessions" and then to receive, from the papal legates, their sentences of imprisonment for life. Instead, these two top officials of the Order of Knights Templar withdrew their confessions and protested to the assembled thousands their own innocence and that of their order. King Philip the Fair did not wait to consult the Pope. He had de Molay and de Charnay burned at the stake the next day in front of the Cathedral of Notre Dame. According to legend, Jacques de Molay, as he burned to death, called down a curse upon the king and his descendants, to the thirteenth generation, and in his last words he summoned king and Pope to meet with him before God's judgment seat within a year. Pope Clement V died within a month and King Philip within seven months. This entire episode, played out before crowds of Parisians, had a profound effect on medieval minds.

Geoffrey de Charnay, the Templar, was burned at the stake in 1314. Geoffrey de Charny of Lirey, a knight of the king, died in battle in 1356 on the field of Poitiers. In 1353, the latter de Charny obtained a grant from King John the Good with which to build the collegiate church of Lirey, a modest wooden structure. It is believed that he had in his possession, at that time, the Turin Shroud, which the Templar de Charny had given him for safekeeping during the period just prior to the breakup of the Order of Knights Templar. There is no proof of a blood relationship between the two knights, despite the similarity in the spelling of the names and the fact that these were not common names in France.

It is believed that Geoffrey de Charny built the Lirey church, near Paris, in order to house the Shroud, but he died on the field of battle a few months after the church was completed. De Charny never admitted publically to owning the Shroud. It is thought that he was unwilling to display it until he had the opportunity to explain adequately to the church authorities how he had come to own a relic intimately related to the Crucifixion and its relationship to the savage downfall of the Knights Templar.

After Geoffrey de Charny's death, his widow, Jeanne de Vergy, found that his beloved foundation, the Lirey church, was an expensive luxury that she could not afford. In consultation with the clergy of the Lirey church, she decided that they should display the Shroud as a means of attracting pilgrims and thereby raising money to maintain the structure. A souvenir medallion was struck, circa 1357, for sale to the pilgrims. One of these medallions was found in the Seine in Paris during the nineteenth century. It includes both the frontal and dorsal images of the Shroud. On the left is represented the shield of Geoffrey de Charny and on the right the arms of Jeanne de Vergy. The roundel in the center represents the empty tomb. Above these is the full-length representation of the Shroud. This is the first extant full-length portrayal of the Shroud. It can be viewed in the Cluny Museum in Paris. Jeanne de Vergy and the Lirey clergy did not inform the bishop or other higher church officials of their intention to display the Shroud. The local bishop, Henry of Poitiers, was incensed and ordered that all exhibitions should cease. His order was based on advice from "many theologians and other wise persons," * who told him that this could not be the real shroud, because it was not mentioned in the Gospels, and that it was a mere painting. Jeanne de Vergy and the Lirey clergy did not know, or at least would not say, how her husband had acquired this very valuable relic of the Passion. The Shroud was withdrawn from display by Jeanne.

Some thirty-two years later, Geoffrey de Charny's son, also named Geoffrey, displayed the Shroud in Lirey, but this time he obtained the permission of the Pope, Clement VII. In order to avoid the type of controversy that arose during the prior exposition of the cloth, Geoffrey II and the Pope agreed to claim it was only an image or likeness and omit any direct claim that it was the true burial cloth of Jesus.

Geoffrey II, the son, made the same mistake that his mother had made in not informing the local bishop, Pierre d'Arcis, of his intention to display the Shroud. The bishop became angry when he learned that large crowds were going to the Lirey church to view the relic. He wrote a note to the Pope, repeating what his predecessor had said about discovering "the fraud and how the said cloth had been cunningly painted, the truth being attested by the artist who had painted it, to wit, that it was a work of human skill and not miraculously wrought or bestowed." The artist, however, was never named. Neither bishop conducted an investigation regarding the cloth. Pope Clement VII

*Memorandum from Bishop Pierre d'Arcis to Pope Clement VII as translated in Appendix B of The *Shroud of Turin*, by Ian Wilson, rev. ed. (Garden City, N.Y.: Doubleday, 1979).

ordered Bishop d'Arcis never to mention the matter again.

From the 1390s to the present, many have believed the Shroud to be a fourteenth-century forgery, based on the d'Arcis memorandum to the Pope. The lack of knowledge about the whereabouts of the cloth prior to the 1350s lent support to the belief that it was a medieval painting. It was not until the twentieth century that scientists were able to prove that the Shroud image is not a painting. The Shroud's history, prior to the 1350s, was not generally known until the British historian Ian Wilson published his book *The Shroud of Turin* in 1978.

Part 11
Paris to Turin via Chambery

The Shroud continued to be displayed on feast days and for other special events in the small wooden church in Lirey, near Paris, until 1418. At that time, the de Charny family was represented by Margaret, daughter of Geoffrey de Charny II. Her first husband had been killed at the Battle of Agincourt in 1415. After Agincourt, the French countryside was ravaged by marauding bands of ex-soldiers and others, to the extent that Margaret felt it was no longer safe to leave the Shroud in the Our Lady of Lirey church. The clergy, therefore, turned the cloth and other jewels and relics of the church over to Margaret and her new husband for safekeeping. There was a promise to return these treasures when law and order were restored in France.

After twenty years of marriage to her second husband, Margaret was still childless. Our Lady of Lirey church, a modest wooden structure to begin with, was in a deplorable state of repair, which caused Margaret to decide to not return the Shroud there. Because she had no direct heirs or any other close relatives that she trusted enough to care for the Shroud, Margaret decided to sell it to Duke Louis Savoy, a member of the powerful and pious House of Savoy. This family was directly descended from Saint Louis, king of France, and had also produced a pope, Felix V, who had reigned as duke but had never been a priest. Margaret felt that Anne and Louis, as rulers of the duchy of Savoy, could provide the security that the Shroud required. This turned out to be a wise decision, as evidenced by the care given the Shroud for over 500 years, from 1453 to 1983, when it was willed to the Vatican upon the death of the former king Umberto II.

Margaret received a castle and revenues from an estate from Duke Louis of Savoy. She also received an excommunication for not returning the Shroud to the church of Lirey. This, however, was lifted after her half brother negotiated compensation to Lirey for the loss of the cloth. Margaret died the next year and apparently compensation was not paid by the de Charny family, but some five years later, Duke Louis assigned fifty gold francs to the Lirey canons in compensation for the loss of the Shroud.

The Savoy family brought the Shroud to Chambery, which was the capital of their dukedom. There they enlarged the ducal church, which was renamed the Sainte Chapelle of the Holy Shroud. The Pope issued a bull setting aside May 4 as the Feast Day of the Holy Shroud. In this and other ways, the House of Savoy raised the status of the Shroud, as compared with the Lirey period, when the de Charnys had difficulty having it displayed.

In the early years after acquiring the Shroud, the son of Pope Felix V Duke Louis, and Anne, the duke's wife, traveled about Europe with the cloth and a retinue of Franciscan friars.

In 1532, some thirty years after the Shroud was placed in the Sainte Chapelle, the fire mentioned earlier in this book broke out in the chapel sacristy. The extensive burn marks that disfigure the cloth were caused by molten silver from the box in which it was kept. The box was doused with water that saved the Shroud but stained it. The holes burned in the cloth by the molten silver were repaired by some Poor Clare nuns. The patches, added by the nuns, and the water stains can be seen on the Shroud today. The scorch marks around the patches, although disfiguring, were useful in the recent scientific evaluation of the Shroud image.

Another threat to the Shroud was a series of invasions by French troops in 1535. The cloth, therefore, was taken to Vercelli and to Nice, which at that time were a part of the duchy of Savoy. By 1561, it was safe to return the Shroud to its refurbished chapel in Chambery.

The duchy of Savoy straddled the Alps, with part in France and part in Italy. After the invasions of the dukedom, mentioned above, the House of Savoy decided that Chambery was not a suitable capital. They decided to cross the Alps and locate the ducal headquarters in Turin among their Italian-speaking subjects. A chapel was built to house the Shroud of Turin in the 1580s. This chapel housed the Shroud until the latter part of the seventeenth century. A magnificent replacement, in the Piedmontese Baroque style, was completed in 1694. There the Shroud has resided to this day. This royal chapel is connected to the ancient Turin Cathedral of Saint John the Baptist and by a tunnel to the royal palace of the Savoys.

The Shroud, when not on display, is rolled around a wooden staff and enclosed in a long, narrow silver chest. It is then locked in a vault behind a grille within a huge monumental altar. Above the altar is an ornate dome that towers above the dome of the Cathedral of Saint John the Baptist. During the Shroud's four hundred–year stay in Turin (except for six years during World War II), it has been on display only twenty times.

In 1861, Duke Victor Emmanuel II became the king of modern Italy. The Savoy's ruled Italy until 1946, when a plebiscite determined that the people preferred a republic. Umberto II went into voluntary exile in Portugal, without being deposed or abdicating. The Savoy palace is now a public museum, and the Shroud was left in the custody of the archbishop of Turin until Umberto's death, when it was willed to the Pope.

An amateur photographer, Secondo Pia, made the first photographs of the cloth in 1898. This opened up the entire field of scientific inquiry into the authenticity of what had been merely an interesting, but controversial religious relic. In the twentieth century, at a time when Catholic historians were beginning to update the image of the church by writing off religious relics as perhaps an unfortunate carryover from less sophisticated times, science was finding that the Shroud could not be so easily dismissed. William F. Buckley, Jr., editor-in-chief of the conservative *National Review* and a Roman Catholic, wrote in the November 27, 1981 edition (p. 1397).

During the past five years the Shroud of Turin has come out of the closet. It has crossed the epistemological threshold into public consciousness, moved from largely religious circles into the major media. . . . The epistemological catalyst, fittingly enough, has been modern science and technology. Science, which powerfully attacks our conception of reality, now attacks the central presuppositions of modern secularism. . . . [The Shroud of Turin Research Project scientists] have brought to bear on the Shroud all of the relevant advanced technology, much of it derived from the space program; computers, image analysers, microscopy, chemical analysis.

To a degree of probability that would have impressed David Hume, the Shroud of Turin strongly indicates that the Gospel narrative is, well . . .true. It looks as if we may actually possess a kind of photograph of the Resurrection. Christians, of course, do not doubt that the Resurrection occurred—although a photograph to buttress that faith is no triviality. But we may also be about to witness widespread and momentous recognition that secularism as a world view is kaput.*

The *New York Times,* in an editorial on December 4, 1981, was somewhat more restrained in its appraisal:

Is the Shroud of Turin the real burial cloth of Christ? The relic, which first appeared about 1350 and is now kept in the Cathedral of Turin, is fast becoming a wonder of this scientific age. There are regular reports, the latest in *Harper's,* about experts who have used the most sophisticated instruments to examine the material and its striking full-length back-and-forth image of a crucified man. The scientists say they can neither prove the Shroud to be a forgery nor account for how it was made, thus leaving the strong impression that it may be the real thing.

But historians note that Europe in the Middle Ages was swamped with purported relics of all kinds. The authenticity of the shroud was questioned from the moment it appeared. At its first exhibition, in 1357, the Bishop of Troyes, France, decided it was a fraud. According to one of his successors, the bishop "discovered the fraud and how the said cloth had been cunningly painted, the truth being attested by the artist who had painted it, to wit, that it was a work of human skill and not miraculously wrought or bestowed."

Because of growing interest in the shroud, the church authorities in Turin have recently allowed certain scientific tests to be made, though not the carbon-14 dating test. Walter McCrone, the Chicago microsocopist who demonstrated that the allegedly pre-Columbian Vinland map of America was a modern forgery, has found evidence of two pigments used in medieval Europe in particles lifted off the shroud. "I am now willing to say that it is an artist's work," he states.

Other tests have found unusual features in the image on the shroud, which apparently cannot be duplicated by modern techniques. But today's technology cannot do everything that yesterday's could—like make violins as well as Stradivarius. We excel over our medieval forebears in many things, no doubt, but should try not to outdo them in credulity.*

In response to the above editorial, the Rev. Vincent J. Donovan wrote a letter to the editor, which was published in the *New York Times* on December 12, 1981:

To the Editor:

The Dec. 4 editorial "The Shroud of Turin" presented two objections to the authenticity of the Holy Shroud: one from the Bishop of Troyes, France, (in 1389) and the other from Dr. Walter McCrone, Chicago, 1981.

According to the editorial, the Bishop said that a previous bishop, in 1357, after an investigation of the shroud "discovered the fraud and how the said cloth had been cunningly painted, the truth being attested by the artist who had painted it, to wit, that it was a work of human skill and not miraculously wrought or bestowed."

The quote is from a letter Bishop Pierre wrote (1389), in anger, to anti-Pope Clement VII, objecting to the exhibition of the shroud at Lirey. He was annoyed because crowds were going to the Lirey chapel and because the shroud's owner, the Charny family, had bypassed him and obtained permission for the exhibit from the papal legate.

Bishop Pierre, at one time a canon lawyer, who would certainly have known the importance of evidence, did not present then, or at any subsequent time, even a single document to support his allegation. A search of the diocesan archives of Troyes failed to turn up any document to show that Bishop Henri, in 1357, ever had the alleged investigation. Pierre died in 1395 and no subsequent bishop ever referred to the incident again. In the space of almost 600 years, no other document has ever come to light to substantiate Pierre's allegations. (Anyone can read a full account of this incident in the scholarly and definitive book "Self-Portrait of Christ," by Father Wuenschel, and then see where he thinks the truth lies.)

As for Dr. McCrone, his published statements as to the shroud being a forgery are shot through with errors and inaccuracies. It should be made clear that he was not in the testing room at Turin in 1978; but, after the American scientists returned to the U.S., Dr. McCrone borrowed about 15 "sticky tape samples" from them. He said: "I believe the shroud is a fake, but I cannot prove it." That, in itself, is a very weak position.

The American team of 27 scientists examined the whole cloth for five days and nights (120 hours) with four tons of the latest space-age scientific equipment. They have asserted (1) that the 3-D negative image on the surface fibrils of the cloth is not a painting; there is no pigment or binder on the cloth; (2) that the iron oxide Dr. McCrone speaks of has nothing whatever to do with the image; (3) that the bloodstains, which are positive, still contain hemoglobin and properties of dried blood.

No artist, even with a photograph as a model, has ever been able to duplicate the shroud and the scientists tell us that there is no method known to modern science by which it can be duplicated. One of them said: "If our testing proved it was a fraud, we would have gone out the door long ago." Dr. Don Lynn of the Jet Propulsion Lab said: "If the shroud is a forgery, it is a greater miracle than if it is real."

The closing sentence of the editorial said that we should not try to outdo our medieval forebears "in credulity." The person who has a thorough knowledge of the detailed markings on the shroud and still says "it is a painting" would be going contrary to an overwhelming mountain of scientific, medical and historic evidence and would be more credulous than those who believe that this mysterious image came somehow from a human body.

(Rev.) Vincent J. Donovan
Pastor, St. John's Church
Oswegeo, N.Y., Dec. 6, 1981

Whether the body image on the Shroud is that of Jesus Christ cannot now be proven, but there is much circumstantial evidence that it is.